Death on the Blue Ocean

RICKARD DAMM

MATTHEW DOERNER-MILLER

Illustrations by Tim Kirby

ISBN: 1492836109
ISBN-13: 978-1492836100

To Debbie and Jennifer - Risk mitigation in the workplace is our specialty. Risk mitigation in our relationships is not. Thank-you of course for your support.

CONTENTS

Part Four – Your Game Plan

Part Five – K.I.S.S (Keep It Simple Stupid)

Prologue

Inspired By True Events

Late Spring, 1668

Alexander Tolliver stared wearily at the unused oars lying at his feet.

Just the thought of raising one from its resting place made the cracks on his bone-dry palms deepen. Each gentle rock of the small boat tore at his aching bones, and each ray of sun tunneled at his cracked lips. *How did it come to this?* he wondered. *How did it all go wrong?*

***

Alexander Tolliver's early career, prior to becoming captain of his very own vessel, was quite average at best. He had not excelled, nor was seen as insufficient, in any specific area of his early education. Because of this, he attended a series of solid, yet generally undistinguished institutions later in his educational career. And while Tolliver did reasonably well with his studies, he did nothing of particular significance that would make him stand out amongst his peers.

As with most that do not have the opportunity to flourish at a prestigious school, upon graduation many of the top-tier companies and enterprises within his local area were simply not within his reach. He and his fellow graduates were destined, so it seemed, to fill the ranks of the middle streets and slightly darkened doorways of the cities and towns of their births and upbringings. Yet Tolliver dreamed still, and his dreams, as it turned out, were the most ambitious of them all.

Along the coastline of the country of his birth, the gray, cold waters of the Atlantic sent shivers down the spines of those who stood along its shores. But to Tolliver, these waters held something more. He knew that beyond the pale waters and sharp winds lay a sea so blue it was rumored to be indistinguishable from a cloudless noon sky. Unlike the heavily trafficked and dangerous waters to the east, full of ships and pirates and rocky traps, the sun washed soft and warm over the gentle rolling waves in this place and held barely another ship for miles. These seas were for the taking.

Having been raised in the paleness of a city's outskirts, deep within the heart of the country, Tolliver had no knowledge of the sea. He knew most everything about plows and harvests and coops and spring plantings, yet his only understanding of the sea was based on the accounts of explorers from long ago. And while he appreciated these stories, the tales of those who searched the red oceans of the Asian coastline, he wanted to embark on something that was without peer and without equal.

From this sea of his dreams, Tolliver knew that he would find the fruits of his undertaking. Lands were rumored to be abundant in all foods and goods, and because the local inhabitants were unaccustomed to seeing people from across the far sea, they were eager to trade goods with these lucky sailors. Although Alexander Tolliver had come from relatively unimportant insignificant beginnings, he spent every waking hour trying to determine how it would be that he could indeed achieve his dream of sailing this ocean of bluest blue.

And then one day, fate finally came to the doorstep of Alexander Tolliver, and under the most peculiar of circumstances.

While languishing in a career of low-level politicking, Tolliver began to pass the time and attempted to erase his growing self-doubt and unease about forever being trapped in the recesses of obscurity, within the arms of a secret lover — a noblewoman, in fact. Though some would say that her dubious affair left her with very little nobility intact.

The Countess de Shurbon was a woman 15 years his senior, and while he could not quite remember how he came to know the countess nor how the affair began, he certainly remembered how it ended.

One evening, as Tolliver and the countess were saying their twilight goodbyes, a rainstorm erupted unlike any that had been seen in recent years. And as Tolliver was attempting a quiet escape up the path and down the now-muddied roadside from the countess's manor, a crashing tree made him leap without pause and forethought, landing him deep within a quagmire of old manure and new mud.

While cursing his luck and attempting to retrieve himself from the mess, he was abruptly struck by the passing coach of the Count de Shurbon himself, who was also returning from a secret midnight rendezvous and was driving his team of horses in an extremely inebriated state (a state for which he was quite well known) — all the while forgetting that his mistress was asleep inside the very carriage that he was driving home.

Embarrassed that his indiscretion had been discovered and fearful about the financial damages that could be awarded to Tolliver based upon his injuries, the count quickly swore an oath to assist Tolliver in the near future, should he have any business or need. And as Tolliver was anxious to accelerate his career and gain access to those of substantial financial means, he immediately requested employment from the count.

Tolliver was given the task of assessing financial damages awarded to noblemen, and he quickly gained a reputation amongst the nobility as one who "accomplishes tasks with expedience and assertiveness." The sky, it seemed, was suddenly the limit for Alexander Tolliver.

Which is why, on that fateful Tuesday morning, Tolliver anticipated no possibility for failure. As his crew let loose the bowlines and the impressive brigantine eased itself through the harbor, Tolliver felt that this moment was meant only for him.

Finally able to assert moderate levels of pressure on those with significant means, Tolliver had begun to petition his wealthy friends on the virtues of his dreams and on the business opportunities of exploring the unexplored oceans. Eventually his impassioned arguments and well-reasoned plans began to have an effect, and he soon secured the necessary investments he required to begin his journey.

Because his wealthy backers — too numerous to list and not without their own demands for his success — had given him more than he needed in terms of supplies, Tolliver wanted to return home with many of the supplies intact to showcase his high level of prudence and shrewdness.

A less welcome contribution from his financers, however, were their four representatives that they insisted accompany Tolliver on his journey. And as they were backing his entire venture, Tolliver could hardly deny their request. Serving no purpose other than to document the journey and provide guidance to the young Tolliver, they were an unfortunate yet necessary nuisance.

His crew of 15 hardened sailors had worked much less impressive brigantines than the one he had secured. His passenger list of 25 included a renowned doctor, a botanist, and several able-bodied carpenters and craftsmen. He had professional cooks and top-notch lieutenants. His team was as complete as one that had ever set out upon the open sea.

***

As he sat in this place of cursed calm, Alexander Tolliver could not understand what had gone wrong. He had formed an appropriate team, and had secured more than enough finances. He had all of the necessary equipment, and he had labored over the plan exhaustively. Everything had been assessed, analyzed, and adjusted for. Yet there he sat floating. Alone.

While the journey had begun exactly on schedule, and the first several weeks had passed according to plan, the trip soon became fraught with unforeseen incidents and problems. And while Tolliver had done his best to remain on task, crew and passenger pressure began to build and questions were raised as to the validity of the journey. As time had been lost to repairs and illness, the four representatives of the financiers argued that a change of course would be needed to make up for lost progress. Although Tolliver initially dismissed their demands, he soon began to tire from their relentless pressure. Eventually even he too began to doubt his plan — the one he had so tirelessly labored over for so many years — and opted to sail into the unknown of the unknown.

The first to fail were the brigantine's sails, as even though they were torn and battered, they had no wind to encourage them along anyways. The next were the arms of the men, who though strong, had lost their motivation and drive and tired quickly of rowing through the thick waters. After the crew went, the extra supplies soon followed - once considered as added luxuries and waste - now were exhausted completely. As the supplies dwindled, so too did the hope of Tolliver's passengers.

Led by his financier's representatives, his team eventually revolted and cast him off his ship — the one he had secured and that his dreams had built. His supplies, once thought to be unnecessary in amount and abundance, had run dry. His ship, once proud and strong and without equal, had sprung leaks within the leaks themselves. His course was lost and his dreams as listless as his unfurled sail. Even waves that lapped against the rotten hull of the rowboat seemed to splash as far away from him as they could manage. He was lost, and only failure could fill his angry, empty stomach. Alexander Tolliver had sailed his dreams directly into the Doldrums, and there they would stay — with no wind, no will, and no way of escape.

PART ONE

Failure is Always Epic

Chapter 1 - Introduction

When we first heard the real story behind the tale of Alexander Tolliver, something immediately bothered us. Finally, after several individual internal debates while stuck in dragging 405 traffic, the significance took shape. Tolliver's dreams were no different than our own—he wanted to explore, to seek adventure, and to seek meaning. He was a man who did not display an innate ability to succeed during his upbringing but who possessed a powerful drive to do something great in his life, at least once.

Although Tolliver's tale took place long ago, we can still draw threads of comparison between his experience and our world today. Our senior management would be his patrons and financial backers. Hear them cry out in angst, "We have to be more like our competition" and "Dare to explore." Ring a bell?

So how are you, a corporate entrepreneur (intreprenuer), similar to Tolliver? Tolliver developed a strong plan, raised more than enough capital, and formed a great team, yet he still failed miserably. Why was this the case, and why is this often the case with corporate ventures today? Is it just bad luck? Too many unforeseen circumstances? Poor execution? These are all common and perhaps perfectly valid reasons why business failures occur. But something still does not make sense. What about those companies that know how to execute and plan for all eventualities, sometimes in absurdum (Coca Cola, Boeing, etc.). There must be something more to it. Things don't just repeatedly happen by coincidence. Somewhere along the line an incorrect decision was made.

Let's start by dissecting exactly how a typical mid-size or larger company is run and how decisions are usually made.

Distilling the decision-making process down to a few simple and generally viable concepts is, of course, impossible. But that won't prevent us from trying. And by "us," we of course mean "them," as in the noble and wise scholars of the ivory tower establishments around the world who spend their time teaching, modeling, and philosophizing about decision-making processes. Teaching and preaching the vintage and well known management models of Five Forces and Blue Oceans will work, financially at least, for the fine academic institutions of this planet who publish the books and sell us the courses on how to "manage" great companies and innovation processes. But do they work in a practical sense for the rest of us?

The average decision-making theory in large companies will most likely produce…an average outcome. Average in terms of financial returns for the company and average in terms of successful corporate ventures. Large companies and the managers within them are usually conditioned to make average decisions and produce average outcomes.

"How can you claim such a thing," you ask? "Insulting us like that! My company only hires the very best, and our strategy is to outperform our competition."

Well guess what — that's also what your competition says.

On the back of a napkin, work out your recent historical performance in terms of P/E and extrapolate into the future with the addition of a little risk premium for market corrections and other potential unknowns. The value of your company, like all other companies, is based on an extrapolation (expectation) of average historical performance combined with an assessment of future Market Risk or Technology Risk.

And there it is. Risk. In truth, managers of any given corporation are there primarily to keep you from screwing up what is already in place. You could perhaps claim that the senior executives' main task is to make sure that the company sticks to its average trajectory while minimizing any downside risk, all the while hoping to fall back-assward into a rocket ship opportunity. Yes, and people do win the lottery, too.

If you invest your money in a large company, a blue chip stock, you would most likely want the managers of the company to first and foremost protect your investment so that you at the very least don't lose your money, correct? In addition you of course hope that they make an above average return; i.e. the balancing act between high risk and possibility of high returns vs. perceived-to-be guaranteed average returns. A bit counterintuitive isn't it, because everybody can't be average.

Companies that steadily perform on an average tangent and boast the occasional above-average return are seen as the best investments. Does this also mean that average people are employed by these same companies?

Yes. Large companies are generally run by average people with average intelligence and average CVs, with the exception of a few outliers.

And yet *risk* is the main driver of decisions in these companies.

Corporate managers are conditioned to eliminate and mitigate risk because ultimately that's the way they are measured and rewarded. If a CEO of a publicly traded company screamed out an annual general meeting that from now on, all his middle managers would be conditioned to take more risks, what do you think the reaction would be? Nervous looks and a tanking share price. So how does the average manager and average employee go about assessing risk?

We are taught to assess risk in our business endeavors every single day. We are trained to be risk conscious. We are bombarded with management literature. We are pointed to blogs and boards on Technology Risk. We listen to podcasts on Market Risk. And we attend courses and conferences and consultations on merging and mitigating and managing risk. Yet still we seem to be missing something. We should have it all covered by now. Failing is not part of any venture's business plan, and yet it still happens all the time.

Shikhar Ghosh, a senior lecturer at Harvard Business School, stated that if failure is defined as failing to meet your original business plan's projections, then more than 95% of start-ups fail. Furthermore, according to a study by Thomas Thurston, as many as 9 out of 10 corporate ventures (large company incubations), fail to stay alive over an extended period of time (more than a couple of business cycles). Failure in business isn't just occurring — it's an epidemic.

***

After even deeper traffic jams and wasted hours on the asphalt, the idea really began to take hold. What if there was a third risk? A shadowy figure that has stalked board rooms since the dawn of business analysis. Forever lurking in the corners of offices and behind water coolers, it has remained unseen and thus unrevealed. Until now.

This book will cover a pragmatic framework for quick and accurate corporate risk management and how to use this analysis to your own personal advantage. In addition to our coverage on how to assess and understand the obvious risks of building a new technology and/or entering new markets, we unmask the shadowy figure mentioned above. A third dimension of risk that will kill even the best of corporate ventures, that many simply, and rather sloppily, refer to dismissively as "office politics". Our ThirdRisk® framework includes an assessment model of this third dimension (TRAC) and several chapters focusing on key mitigation and execution principles.

Many successful leaders master the ThirdRisk® intuitively. However, these successful leaders will very seldom, when it is time to sum up their careers with a ghost-written autobiography, tell you the stories about how they managed to outmaneuver and defeat their office antagonists. Or how they intentionally sub-optimized their kingdom in order to better appeal to top management, rather than striving to do what would have been beneficial for the company on the whole. Instead you will read things like "work harder than everybody else and success is imminent" or "A players hire A players and B players hire C players – be an A player!" Seriously? We understand that we live in a culture of snack-size consumables and sound bites, but this type of tripe is just plain insulting.

At least buy us dinner before you screw us.

Rather than bumbling our way through 200 pages of "success comes to the prepared and agile" corporate jargoning, we'll play Penn & Teller for a bit. We will show you how to make a more accurate and realistic assessment of risk than any Ivy League MBA or senior executive down the hall. We will also show you how to become a better decision maker when it comes to analyzing new venture opportunities, and how to play in the corporate political major league.

A note to our more critical readers out there: this book is not a dissertation, nor is it meant to usurp any specific model. In fact, much of what we cover here is simply a bastardized and puréed mix of advanced management literature. Think of it as your morning power shake. We didn't invent the ingredients — just the combination.

We have created an experienced-based and weather-tested model for pragmatically managing corporate assignments, and we believe this model could have a huge impact on your career. As company executives, we have seen buckets of both failure and success, and we take pride in trying to make different mistakes each time we venture out into something new. So relax and take this book for what it is: a framework for becoming a respected and successful intrapreneur.

Chapter 2 - The Fallacy of Adopting Entrepreneurial Modeling

Vomit in the mouth. This is what we do every time a new book or blog extols the virtues of "being more entrepreneurial" within an organization. Entrepreneurial "throw spaghetti at the wall and see what sticks" models and frameworks are not meant to be used in larger organizations. In fact, we challenge you to name one large, traditionally structured company that suddenly became more "entrepreneurial." And we don't mean a large company that cleaned out some dusty bottom floor, added fresh paint, and created an open floor plan. We mean some 1980s Gordon Gekko-meets-Mad Men operation that suddenly did a complete 180 and changed its entire structure to become leaner and more open.

That's what we thought.

Just as "going green" was all the rage during the mid-90s, with every CSR campaign belaboring the fact that "the office now has two, count them, two recycling bins", it is trendy today to define one's corporate identity as "entrepreneurial." It is sort of like someone telling you that they are a born-again virgin—you might hear the words, but deep down you call bullshit.

So what is the problem with entrepreneurial frameworks? The obvious answer is that they were built in an attempt to solve a different problem. They have been modified to help budding entrepreneurs scale nearly insurmountable obstacles, such as a lack of funding, an underdeveloped team, or an undefined market window.

The real problem arises when one dopey senior manager does his or her dopey senior manager math and builds something like the following:

Product (Investment + Team + Market Window) / (Risk x Probability) = Corporate Big Hairy Audacious Goal (BHAG)

Then the dopey senior manager takes this dopey senior management framework and does what he or she normally will do when stuck on a problem: Googles "management frameworks for dopey senior managers who are trying to expedite product development and delivery." And because the Google search algorithm is at the mercy of the dopey senior manager's input, it spits out a lot of information based on specific keywords.

Suddenly something catches the dopey senior manager's eye. "Expedite" and "product" and "development" pop up in the 150-character search results.

"Everything I wanted is right here on the first article of the first page!" exclaims the dopey senior manager. Boom goes the dynamite.

Product (Investment + Team + Market Window) / (Risk x Probability) = My Interpretation of an Entrepreneurial Framework

The next thing you know, this same dopey senior manager is handing out dozens of copies of the entrepreneurial equivalent to *Everyone Poops* and telling you that based on this research, you must become much more . . .

. . . entrepreneurial.

Cue vomit.

This, of course, is the obvious example of why these frameworks don't work. Now we will talk a little bit about the giant purple elephant in the room that makes everyone uncomfortable. The less obvious and more sinister reason why these frameworks do not apply to the larger, more traditional organization is because large, traditional organizations do not attract employees with deep-seated entrepreneurial inclinations.

Let's face it — everyone dreams of owning a pet store/gastropub/surfboard shop. Very, very few of these dreamers ever attempt to pursue said dream. The corporate world does an excellent job of making you feel comfortable. It pays you just enough so that you can barely buy that house. Then it pays you just enough to get married. The next year you scrape enough cash together to feel like you can afford your first child. Then another one. Then college, Christmases, car repairs, and on and on it goes.

Life suddenly takes over. Remember that beer rant you had when you were 30, when you told your friends, "One day soon I'll take the plunge and do my own thing"? Now you're 45 and just hoping not to make too many waves in order to keep your job safe and secure. You've jettisoned your entrepreneurial dreams and have happily exchanged them for moderate security and a paid vacation. The last thing you want or need is some dopey senior manager trying to wrest you from your safe and comfortable spot to make you do something that will surely put a giant target on your back.

Think about some of the greatest entrepreneurs of the recent 2 decades: Mark Zuckerburg (never graduated), Mark Cuban (worked at a company for less than a year before starting his own), Richard Branson (started his first company at 16), and Steve Jobs (dropped out of college after 6 months). Each one had a very brief taste of what it was like to work for someone else before deciding quite definitively that it was not for him. And while we understand that these are extreme examples, think about your reasons for taking, or more importantly staying at, your first then second then third job. Why don't you have the same visceral reaction about "working for the man"? Maybe, just maybe, you aren't quite as entrepreneurial as you would like to think you are.

In the past, this may not have been a big deal, but as companies increasingly beat the entrepreneurial war drum, that safe little cubicle down at the far end of the hall no longer feels so safe. Someday soon, a decree will be issued. You will be asked to develop ideas about how your group can become more "innovative" and "lean." You might need to write a report on what the hell "Operational Excellence" actually means and use it to inspire your fellow colleagues (though everyone knows that these types of reports aren't good for much outside of lining the cage of a diarrheic hamster). The very job security that you have come to appreciate is now at risk because the company has suddenly become caught up in the euphoria and rhetoric of becoming more entrepreneurial. Crap.

So what do you do? You are not interested in disrupting the market, and you are especially not eager to run a new rogue business unit. But if you say no or, even worse, nothing at all, your progression within the organization could be at risk. In short—how can you appease your bosses and excel at a game that you aren't really keen on playing in the first place?

The questions above are a few obvious examples of things never covered by typical business school planning templates. While we may be sounding a little pessimistic in our claims, the fact of the matter is that showcasing the truth (internal political strive and administrative risk) in new ventures will never get your name in lights. You won't win any Nobel prizes, your book sales will be abysmal. Perhaps most dreadful of all, you will sell a grand total of zero management consulting hours if you preach this gospel. It is far more lucrative to be the supposed rock star, swaggering about with your Devil-may-care haircut and your strategically mismatched attire, talking about how there are blue oceans of profits just waiting to be explored. You just need to simply try harder apparently.

Chapter 3 - The Glam Rock Curve

"Hellllllooo Cleveland!" BOOM BOOM go the drums. *"You ready to rock?"* you shout.

You strut across the stage in your ripped tights and studded vest. Your glam rock hair bounces with every swing of your hips, and your lips slightly pucker with each heel click of your red pleather cowboy boots.

"LEAN!" you call out. The crowd goes nuts.

"DISRUPTIVE!" you shriek. Lighters raise to the air.

"INCUBATING-BUSINESS-BARTER-DRILL-DOWN-METRIC-VALUATION-BLUE-SKIES-RED-OCEAN-TOO-MANY-CHIEFS-AND-NOT-ENOUGH-INDIANS-VALUE-CHAIN-DISRUPTION-SEED-CAPITAL-ANGEL-FUNDED-30-SECOND-3-SLIDE-ELEVATOR-SCRUM-SANDBOX-GAMIFY-THE-PROCESS-PAAARRRYTY PEOPLE!"

The girls faint and the boys cry. And you walk off without ever singing a single original note.

There seems to be a glut of en-vogue "entrepreneurs" these days. Anyone who has the ability to sift through grandma's couch cushions can come up with $10 in pennies and buy a domain name for a new "venture". And then almost as suddenly, he or she is an expert.

Kurt Cobain and Axl Rose, two musical geniuses, hated each other. Why? Kurt apparently loathed the era of rock from which GnR hailed—cheesy outfits, big hair, and anthem ballads. Kurt was trying to take rock music into more introspective territories, and hence, a clash was born.

We are currently in the glam rock era of entrepreneurship. Everybody is playing the same four chords with a giant purple keytar, but the music still sells albums, despite its arguable lack of substance. Sure it's fun, but we should have changed the record ten years ago. And what is even scarier is where we are headed next. Let's just say that we're not real Beliebers in the state of true innovation in the near future.

In business modeling, there are two basic types of new business ideas that can be easily weeded out: those that are weak but easily deployable, and those that are strong but not feasible in the mass market. Neither of these will ever become a sustainable and strong venture. The former because of quickly diminishing returns and the latter due to the sheer lack of an immediate addressable market. If your venture falls within either of these domains you can stop reading right now and head back to the drawing board. Yes, that means you, the inventor and sole proprietor of the *ant-farm-on-demand.com* site. You don't have a big enough market, so go home and rethink.

But, what about the rest of us? What if we have something that might actually be a good idea and could possibly be deployed and built within a reasonable timeframe? This is exactly the problem that the sea of books and the endless hours of lectures try to sell to you as having the answer.

Innov-celebs such as Eric Reiss, Steve Blank, and Alexander Osterwalder have ultimately repackaged traditional models such as Lean (popularized by Toyota Production System and GE 20+ years ago), Five Forces etc. to have more modern connotations and that appeal to the (less academically minded) corporate execs of today. The underlying premise of models such as the Lean Startup and Business Model Generation remains the same — start small, launch early, beta test, build, iterate, and hope that something sticks. It's sort of like cooking spaghetti: you don't take a big clump and throw it at the wall to see if it's ready; you take single strands at different times, and maybe throw them on different spots. While this is fine for the garage start-up, it is not relevant for the in-house corporate project. But yet this is where most of us will ultimately spend our time.

Some lean start-up methods could perhaps be used to create a demo or prototype, but corporate managers are simply not conditioned to allow anyone to experiment with live customers. No matter how good your team is or how little money you will spend or how agile you will work. Your senior managers need to manage their own risks, i.e., cover their own asses. Managers in large companies are there to keep you from employing the lean start-up method and not to support you in your tinkering. Large company middle managers actually have all the reasons in the world (as we will return to later in the book) to prevent you from going down the launch-fast-and-iterate path of innovation. And yet whenever our bosses tell us to be more entrepreneurial, they always point to these types of frameworks and refer to the non-relevant case studies (e.g. Nespresso, Xerox, and Apple) that we all studied in business school. Case studies that in essence tell you how to work faster, more productively, and at a cheaper cost. Case studies that are disproportionate in scope and scale to your situation.

Being a large corporation is fundamentally different from being a start-up. A typical start-up, with its limited resources and reduced market window, cannot have a plan to mitigate all the major sources of risk at the same time. It will not be able to effectively handle the pressures associated with a lack of financial resources and investor patience, while at the same time finding time to educate the market while it is building its new and unproven technology.

In reality, start-ups in a Blue Oceans usually fail. The great new idea slowly and painfully dies the death of being burned from both ends. While trying to develop a new market and encourage customer buy-in, you are also trying to create new technology to answer a question nobody has asked yet. As a start-up, you don't have the time, resources, or ability to handle both technical and market risk at the same time.

What everyone wants to hear about is the exciting path to the pot of gold at the end of the rainbow, not the root that was sticking up in the middle of the path that made you twist your ankle along the way. And while current start-up/entrepreneurial pitches might be encouraged and preached at the Lean Startup conference you were sent to last year, or in that article your manager emailed you last week (think elevator pitches and the 3-slide approach), they are completely wrong within the context of a larger business.

You will most likely never do a *Dragons' Den* pitch over coffee at the Creamery with larger company execs. Instead, you will have to work your way through the political ranks and give 2-hour presentations to a plethora of stakeholders before a decision is made — in many ways the exact opposite of a VC pitch. Your first meetings will likely be the longest and most difficult ones. You better be prepared.

References derived from the blogosphere ("lean start-ups," "customer development," "being agile all the way," "gamifying the development/consumer engagement process") will not resonate with senior managers when used as a crutch during your presentation. Working in a large company comes with its own grind, and its own set of rules. Simply put, don't try to smokescreen a poorly applied model by utilizing en vogue references. At best, you will win the presentation but ultimately lose the battle (as we will show later). At worst, and most likely, you will come across as foolish, unprepared, and naive and will never be called upon again. In short, your moment to shine in front of the career gatekeepers will have been wasted.

So now that we've showed you some of the reasons why you shouldn't rely on entrepreneurial frameworks in their totality when trying to build your risk-adverse intrapreneurial profile, let's talk about where to start developing your business case.

PART TWO

Risk

Chapter 4 - Risk Siloing: The First Steps

In 1999 Harvard and MIT joined forces and created a project that would allow them to look more closely at managing risk in high-tech investment opportunities (typically venture capital or large company investment situations). The end result was a lengthy academic report, a book, and a core 2-by-2 management consultancy–style model.

The basic foundation of the model that was created is as such: if you are thinking of venturing out into a new and unknown area of business, you need to reduce your exposure to both Market Risk and Technology Risk during the development phase of your venture. For the sake of simplicity, think of Market Risk as the "Opportunity Analysis" and Technology Risk as the "Feasibility Analysis".

Say you wanted to launch a new social network in this day and age. It would make sense to first assess the Market Risk. Are there many other social networks currently on the market? Is your offer unique in any way and does it have any specifications that will distinguish it from the rest? Is there even a need for the platform to exist?

All things equal, the best product should win the race, right? The most stable platform with the most flexible and adaptable user interface should make a killing in the market. Additionally, the market is large enough that you only need to appeal to and win 1 percent of the addressable market. In doing so, you will be richer than rich.

"So what's the problem? Let's build now! I'll interrupt the board meeting and breathlessly tell the board to go for it."

Not so fast.

For any opportunity you might think of, there is always someone who has thought of it first. Let's say there are roughly 100,000,000 different things to buy right now — 100,000,000 unique SKUs, of which there are millions of each type. With each of these SKUs comes a salesperson employed at a company. This company is equipped with a marketing department, a chief operating office, legal team, and HR.

You are one of these eager employees pushing 1 of 100,000,000 SKUs. Your new idea is great. Your market sizing is correct. Your channel strategy and marketing mix is simply a work of art; 1 measly percent of the market should be easy enough to win. Even better, if you manufacture and sell it in China, all you need is half a percent. How hard can it be?

Really, really hard. In order to get your new idea approved and funded, your assessment of market size has to be better than your colleague's. You don't have to have any magic powers, but you definitely need to avoid becoming the Mr. Bean of business planning.

Once you have answered the tough questions associated with Market Risk, you must assess the associated Technology Risks. Say you still want to start that social networking platform. Because the concept is not new, there are many models out there from which to garner technical inspiration. So the basic formula in your initial analysis would be:

Social network platform + 2014 = huge Market Risk but small Technology Risk

Now imagine the opposite scenario. You have found the cure for stupid driving by way of administering a single shot to everyone getting their driver's license. There will be little Market Risk, as nothing similar exists in the world and there is an obvious and pressing need for it. Instead, there will be a huge Technology Risk regarding research, development, and delivery of this treatment to all areas afflicted by poor drivers. Here you have a very strong idea, but an extremely daunting plan of attack:

Stupid driving antidote + 2014 = small Market Risk but huge Technology Risk

So which is the greater of the two? Technical or Market risk? Which one should you start with? Based on individual makeup, people will be better at one or the other. And you are no exception.

This book is about taking traditional risk assessment into a more pragmatic and realistic dimension. Put yourself in the shoes of the corporate executive trying to do his or her best to discredit your investment proposal — what is the first thing that you care about above all else? 9 times out of 10 it will be "how fast can I make money." So with this in mind, let's start with practically assessing Market Risk, because the market is where money is made.

Chapter 5 - Market Risk

Many consultants reference the Market and Technology Risk model, yet instructions on how to use it to your advantage are few and far between. While most senior executives intuitively understand the concept, very few actually use this model formally. You need to take their instinctual understanding of these concepts and formalize it in your business case. Ultimately if you use the formalized model, very few top-level managers will be able to challenge your conclusions.

The first step is to attack the Market Risk head-on. The Market Risk assessment is arguably more important to nail than the Technology Risk assessment, since it will address many of the assumptions and preconceptions associated with your basic premise.

Jack: "I will sell 10 billion units of widgets by 2020, thereby capturing 2.6% of the overall market share."

Jill: "No, I think you will reach 2.3% market share, not 2.6% by the end of the period. Can you please explain the assumptions you made to determine your figure?"

Jack begins to panic—nervous coughs, sputters, "umms" and "ahhs." He starts flipping frantically back and forth through his slides in an attempt to prove his undocumented assumptions. He loses the flow of his pitch and fails to sell his business case.

Say you work in a company with lots and lots of engineers who love to geek out over the latest programming script flows and *Dr. Who* episodes. Having the Market Risk dimension top of mind at all times will protect you from becoming too caught up in technical wizardry and enthusiasm, which is very easy to do. You can instantly regain self-control if you feel yourself being swayed by slick depictions of big blinking lights and the tinny voice of the WOPR. Stay away from the light and remain within the dirty, ugly street fight that is the market. You need to figure out and mitigate risk here first, or else everything subsequent will stand on a house of cards.

By now a few of you are thinking, "Wait, wait, wait. This is not true at all. A market does not know or understand what it wants until the technology dictates what it can have and therefore want. Ever hear of Henry Ford or Steve Jobs? The early adopters of new technology set the tone of the market and are the guiding forces that vet or accept each and every new gadget and gizmo that comes to pass. The early adaptors show the rest of society what products we should buy, and we like bad-ass stuff." Or so says the Mountain View glasshole.

The sarcasm might be a little heavy here, but isn't this basically what we have been hearing lately? Isn't this what the technology life cycle models say? Find your early visionary buyers and the rest will follow suit as long as you can cross the "chasm"? Oh and by the way, don't worry about defining exactly what this "chasm" is or how to navigate it — that's for the sales and marketing frameworks to figure out. It's more fun living within the rainbow.

Existing scientific evidence stating that early adopters pave the way for the mass market is actually a little suspect in itself. This idea originates from the concept of a product life cycle, which in turn gravitates around the diffusion of innovation and markets. The funny thing about this, however, is that many of the life cycle studies were done nearly a century ago and most notably address the spread of new farming practices among Iowa corn farmers (Rogers, E. M. 2003. Diffusion of innovations 5th ed.). Are you a corn farmer? In Iowa? Then why do you believe that there is such a thing as early adopters and mass markets? And saying that a voice whispered "if you build it they will come" is not a strong enough reason.

Consider the great success of the iPhone. The first iPhones were bought by the enlightened few. They promoted it to their friends, who also bought iPhones, and so on. A few years down the road, even Granny Matilda has an iPhone. By the product life cycle definition, the iPhone should now be breathing its last breath and Apple should be milking the remainder of the market before the inevitable outcome — death by saturation. Not really the case, is it?

It can be argued (and often is) that as the technology evolved, so did iPhone and its user base. Granny might have been, for a short period of time, an inadvertent early adopter when she upgraded her older phone out of necessity and became one of the first with an iPhone 5S. Get the point here? The market is not the market.

You are in the business of selling gizmos and services to people. You need to find out how many Grannies are going to upgrade the coming year and how many of them you could possibly appeal to at a certain price point. Purchase decisions in this day and age are everything but predictable. 100,000,000 options, remember.

Early geeky adopters may end up creating the new Google, but you might as well have created the new Instagram-for-engineers-at-Google-who-love-pictures-of-purple-frogs. In this demographic (grand total of 6) you will make a killing but will have the challenge of always trying to reach a wider audience. Add up the total number of purple-frog-loving engineers in the world and include their friends and affiliated influencer groups (now you have 11 people), and you have, at the very least, your first shot at your short-term market potential.

"OK, enough ranting. You've convinced us that we should always take Market Risk into consideration first, at least when working with one of you two twits. So now what?"

Of course you need your hockey stick charts and of course you should read the market reports. But more importantly, you should always be ready to answer these two simplest of questions:

1.   Who will your first customer be?
2.   What is this customer's profile?

Let's give you a picture of what a really good market analysis looks like. Take the market for, say, shish kebab flavored ice cream. This has not been marketed before and is clearly a blue ocean with a seemingly huge market (everyone who loves Middle Eastern food and ice cream to start with, right?). The first step is to look at the total ice cream market in your target region. Next, look at how many packages and servings are sold per capita in your target region. Voila — now you have enough information for a very rudimentary (but still presentable) total addressable market slide. This should have taken you a grand total of 5 to 10 minutes, given that you are somewhat knowledgeable about your target market.

Now comes the cool part; find yourself a good first example of a target audience:

Teenage boys, 13–15 years old, who would like shish kebab flavored ice cream a) as a prank or b) because they love the flavor of meat, even in a dessert.

Whatever total you extrapolate will equal your total market size. The next step is to ask yourself how many of these boys will actually pay real money for your ice cream by extrapolating from your per capita finding and then multiplying this with how many times each person will buy this ice cream each year (in this awful example, once, presumably). You now have your initial target market projection, which is your first shot at determining how big your market is among the audience who will give you your first dollar.

In order to take your analysis one step further, you should multiply your projection with the number of other possible target audiences. This will give you a more precise total addressable market size for you new ice cream venture.

This exercise should take no more than a couple of hours, including some Twitter and Facebook procrastination. Take that, you expensive and overrated management consultants. But just like today's high-level consultancy "solutions," this market projection will be exactly as wrong in the end as a consultant's best, and most expensive, shot.

The truth is that the first dollar is the hardest to make. The first $10,000 in sales will equal the effort of the coming $1,000,000. This is partly why we sometimes misinterpret scale. A company and its products don't just magically grow from 0 to 100 with hockey stick statistics. What happens in reality is that a few poor people work their butts off to get the first few orders in order so that top management can run around the world and talk about their great success and sign simple orders. ("Stop complaining you guys; this thing basically sells itself. Just try harder and we will reach another 10 percent growth next year.")

Business managers and decision makers could care less about an idea that cannot generate revenue on the market, nor do they wish to get into a street fight with already established players if the returns are not high enough. Address Market Risk first, and you have already gained their respect. But you haven't yet ensured your victory.

How long will it take to present this type of market projection in your pitch to senior management to gain funding for your new venture? Our best guess is somewhere between 1 and 4 minutes. "What? Market Risk is the most important element! That's what you said."

Yes we did. This is another reason why you should never spend money on management consultants for market projections alone, unless, of course, you happen to be especially moronic and want to spend company funds unwisely. "Still, 1 to 4 minutes for all that work? What will I cover in the rest of the meeting?" Well, let's just say that you now need to get back into your comfort zone of geek-izadry and bring on the technical and functional slides.

Pro Tip

Make aggressive market projections but don't be SpongeBob. If a large "insight" provider or external management consultant assist you with market forecasting, always, we repeat, ALWAYS have a bottom-up perspective. This will allow you to utilize your intrinsic capability to sell and deliver a product.

I have often been guilty of presenting figures that will simply not add up or stand the test of the simplest arguments. For example, if you come presenting your new venture idea to me it could play out something like this.

Me: "How many customers did you say you would have in Year 3, and how long is the typical sales cycle?"

You: "Umm, 100 customers and a sales cycle of 4 months, typically."

Me again: "OK, with an average hit rate of 50 percent, which by far exceeds your current hit rate within the company, and an average meeting frequency of X for each sales guy per week, you would have to have 4 times as many sales guys than are available in the company today. Sorry, but please go back to the drawing board."

Case closed…

(Authors' note: When describing the ThirdRisk® model later in the book, we will address the perfect way to mitigate this situation, but you will never be able to salvage a complete off-the-board calculation like the above example, so, make the numbers stack up.)

Chapter 6 - Technology Risk

You must acknowledge Technology Risk — it's a do-or-die issue.

Without technical disruptions and innovations, the productivity frontier would not be pushed outward. Without Technology Risk, disruptions would never occur and all companies would live forever. Why change, adapt, and create if there is never a real need for it? All companies die sooner or later, usually because some newer, more efficient technologies disrupt them while they stubbornly stick to their helm.

Dystopia once again? Don't worry about it. You should be happy. As an aspiring entrepreneur or intrapreneur, you are, at the very least, punching slightly above your weight and trying to save the day, one small step at a time.

Technology Risk comes in many forms and is very different from Market Risk. If we could decipher the risk and rewards of all potentially disruptive new technologies in the same way we dissect new business models, we would no longer have to do real work for a living.

Nobody can really assess how easy or hard it will be to deliver a new high-quality technology within a certain time frame. The effort involved in realizing your mistakes in your market analysis and changing your business model half way through your venture's startup cycle is not comparable to the effort required when needing to do the same for your underlying technology. Launching your technology platform early and iterating as you go is not always an option, especially if you are putting the good will and faith of existing customers at stake. Which in turn ties back to what we discussed earlier. For innovators in larger organizations, modeling your new business idea on current innovation frameworks is not as valid as the contemporary high priests of business literature claim.

Successful ventures in larger companies often reuse the incumbent business models, at least to start with. Most people understand this intuitively. If you have a variable-cost business model, make sure you have, at the very least, a viable shot at creating a technology that you can scale as you grow and not one that requires a large amount of upfront or tied-in capital. Starting your pitch with "it's-not-built-but-will-be-soon-after-X-amount-of-dollars" is a losing proposition. You will come across as a flake and someone who has not put a lot of effort into real analysis.

Star Trek is epic. Gene Roddenberry created something that transcended generations with its creativity, interesting characters, and fun story lines. But one of its greatest attributes is also its weakest. Writers generally call this the "Star Trek Technology Crutch."

Think about it. Enterprise is in yet another previously unknown area of space, facing yet another previously unknown danger. This Tribble/Khan/Crystalline Entity/Borg/Khan-Again hybrid has Captain Kirk/Picard/Kirk-Again up against the ropes. The ship's shields are down to 5 percent (stop us if this sounds familiar), and one more hit from the Tribble/Khan/Crystalline Entity/Borg/Khan-Again hybrid will mean the certain end of Enterprise forever.

Suddenly, Spock/Data/Spock-Again has an idea. A completely untested hypothesis rendered in sheer chaos in just under 15 seconds could theoretically not only save Enterprise and her crew, but also will most likely solve whatever diplomatic issue created the battle in the first place.

After several more explosions that kill Anonymous Red Shirt Guys 1, 2, 5, and 12, the captain gives his blessing. In less than a minute, a new technology is created from a jerry-rigged version of something that was just lying around on the ship. This something was never spoken about or referenced before and was, up until this point, completely useless — much like a floor lamp or a bag of oranges. Yet in the moment of utter destruction, this floor lamp or bag of oranges, when modified, becomes a bad-ass alien problem solver.

Don't let your Technology Risk assessment sound like a Star Trek ending. Make sure it is concrete, based in reality, and bulletproof.

Corporate decision makers need to see an exponentially larger market potential in order for a disruptive and novel technology to become a viable investment. They will not invest in, or rather gamble on, your "Nespresso for Ketchup" project unless you can prove that you have viable technology (and market sizing) to back it up. But they might, however, approve the "network as a service enabled by a breakthrough software technology" without you necessarily having to be 100 percent certain about the business model — as long as you can prove that this will be cheaper than existing products out there and that you are addressing a large existing market.

So how do you pragmatically address Technology Risk in your intrapreneurial project?

First answer the obvious questions:

1. What is the technology behind the idea?
2. Is there anything else like it currently being developed or on the market?
3. How easily replicable is it?

The last point is double edged. If it's easy, then you don't need that much money, but it shouldn't be that easy, or else you'll be in a knife fight sooner rather than later. It can be tricky to find the perfect balance.

Technology Risk will always depend on a few unique factors representative of your specific setting. What in your company seems like a minor hurdle could be a total roadblock in another. You might be battling to update your Facebook profile picture while others are trying to invent cold fusion.

So first, you need to find your company's baseline. This is not an absolute science, of course, but the process might be more intuitive than you think. There are two main dimensions to consider: "Technical Leap of Faith" and "Achievability".

The Technical Leap of Faith describes how incremental and proven vs. how innovative and unproven your technology is. A totally new and unproven technology is the highest risk, a new technology with proven feasibility is medium risk, and an incremental evolution based on a proven technology is the lowest risk.

Achievability should be viewed in terms of how specified the new development effort is in terms of implementation. And now you need to be very, very cautious not to tread in the muddy waters of the "lean start-up" movement, where Market and Technology Risk are bundled together. For our Feasibility Assessment, we are only looking at ease of implementation and the strength in the underlying understanding of proposed new technology. Modest extension of functionality and natural extension of performance will be low risk; a new specification on top of existing technology with extended performance requirements will be medium risk. A technology and performance that is impossible to specify (invention) will be the highest risk.

Now you have to average out your 2 dimensions and plot them on a scale from low to high. Remember that the scale of Technology Risk can be deceptive. The scale of Technology Risk has a tendency to be exponential in terms of effort to solve the problem at hand. We will return to this when we talk about the ThirdRisk® later in the book. For now, just consider the model's exponentiality a fact of life. Creating a life-changing new technology is harder than you might think.

In our experience, most would-be intrapreneurs fail here. They either keep their evaluations far too simplistic and make wild claims of singularity and uniqueness, or they don't dig deep enough and understand that what they are proposing doesn't warrant such advanced technology. Far too often, when given the challenge and opportunity to explore new business unit avenues, intrapreneurs jump headfirst into solving and developing complicated technological disruptions. This is amateurish. Managers and investment committees are far more impressed if you show some analytical chops by identifying parallel business opportunities and leveraging in-house technology. This is much safer and ultimately much more in line with the comfort zone of traditional companies. First, show them internal synergies that come with an inherent lower risk and cost profile, and you will be rewarded with the right to stake out your technology vision.

Compare Samsung's recent earnings to BlackBerry's. Samsung does not try to reinvent the mobile phone, just the processes and methodology of development, sales, and user experience. BlackBerry keeps whimpering about being the inventors of the smartphone. Which company would you let hold on to your 401(k)? Actually, by the time you read this, the argument might be moot anyways.

Combining the Two

Hail the 2-by-2 model of Market and Technology Risk. We did say that the indisputable truth could be presented in this model, right? The two axes of the model are described above with the Market Risk resting on the vertical axis and Technology Risk on the horizontal. And, in true *Harvard Business Review* style, we have given each quadrant a name:

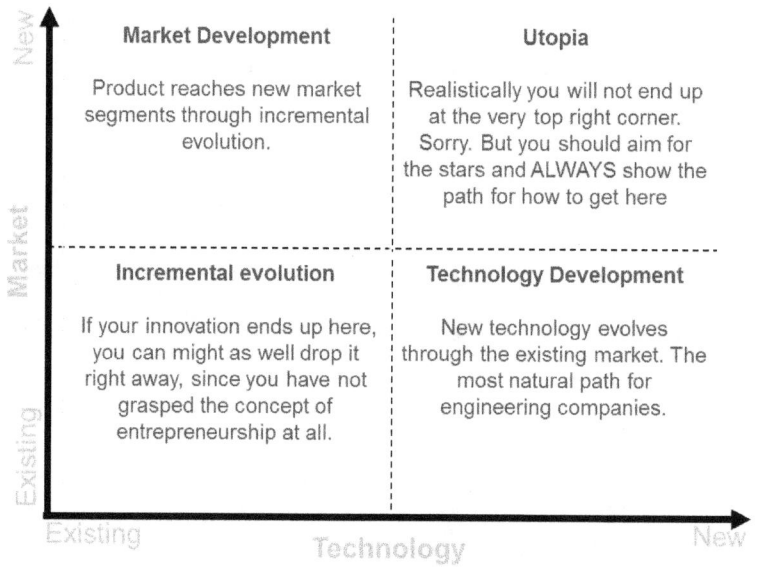

Chart 1: The four quadrants explained. Copyright 2013 - ThirdRisk®

Naturally all managers will want you to end up in the top right quadrant. This is, as in all 2-by-2 models, where the rainbow ends. Here, consumers who are entranced by your magical product bring money into stores with wheelbarrows.

As an intrapreneur in a large company, you can successfully venture into the blue ocean all by yourself. You can actually handle two risks simultaneously. But unlike in a start-up, an inherent problem exists in new ventures within large corporations. While both Market and Technology Risks remain, a third, unseen iceberg is cruising towards your hull.

Pro Tip

Always find great new blue oceans of customers for your company. But in corporate venturing contexts, always create a product that you can validate and sell to existing customers first. This may sound boring and, to a certain extent, counterintuitive in an entrepreneurially focused book. But face it — your company, unless you are GE or maybe Samsung, exists within a certain context. Illusions of brands being totally transferrable have failed over and over again. Don't go there. Don't try to venture into new technologies and new customers at the same time. It will not work. You will be setting yourself up for failure. Stick to ventures that can expand from your core propositions and organizational capabilities. Period. Your first customer for your new product or solution should be an existing customer.

PART THREE

The Missing Piece

Chapter 7 - TRAC Overview

Let's venture into the unknown with the assistance of the ThirdRisk®

model's inner workings. We will start by looking at what this risk

actually consists of. A type of risk that exists in corporations of all sizes,

regardless of location. It lies in wait, ever eager to take a bite out of your

business, your product, and your personal reputation.

Politics. Office politics — a very broad term, but is in essence what

ThirdRisk® is all about. Politics within companies will get the best

projects canceled and the best people fired. However, politics can also

get the worst projects funded and give the biggest morons the corner

office. Office politics must be understood and used to your advantage.

We promise to not go off on a tangent about "beating the system" by

outsmarting your managers or working the 2-hour work week. We know

the power of hard work, and we know that delivering on time and

answering emails at 2:00 a.m. actually, sadly, does influence your career

trajectory. Anyone who tells you differently is selling you the lazy pill.

We also understand and respect the fact that large companies have operational models, strategic planning, and management accounting in place. We will not teach you to game this either. Think of us like guitar teachers. You don't necessarily need to be the best guitar player to become a rock star — you just need to master the basics, play the safe chords, and improve over time. We can provide the simple progressions and a basic beat to fit within your comfort zone. You can play the ThirdRisk® office politics riff without the fear of losing everything by trying to game the system.

Like the diligent management consultant/corporate wizard MBAs we are, we have, of course, crafted our own 4-letter abbreviation to help you remember the important core dimensions of our model. We use this all the time, both as prospective intrapreneurs and investors. We call this TRAC, and it's our reason for writing this book. "Targets", "Resources", "Alignment", and "Communication". TRAC for short.

Now is a good time for us to reiterate what we told you at the beginning of this book: we do not claim to have invented the underlying models. At face value, you can already start to mix and match the words that build the TRAC abbreviation and shout at us that we are full of corporate BS lingo. And maybe we are. But bear with us here. We're not about to tell you how to "align your targets". Or how to "communicate to your resources". That's the easy part. What we will do is to help you assess your risk profile in order to create a winning strategy that will make you come out as a hero.

Assessing and strategizing all your project's political risk elements can be a tedious exercise, so we have tried to abstract TRAC to a level that will enable you to do so in a very short time — maybe less than an hour, maybe even less than a few minutes once you get the hang of it. Shortly, we will address how to work through it practically. First, you will need to actually do the assessment and begin to build your strategy.

Let's dissect each TRAC dimension in order of abbreviation sequence, even though it does not matter which dimension you start with.

Chapter 8 - Targets

Individual or group targets in any given company are somehow what the ring is to Gollum. Targets are created artificially by the gods and handed down on stone tablets. Targets are the lifeblood of a company and the juggernaut of managers. They are incontestable and always hard to reach.

Executives create targets by a) synthesizing a business plan, b) extrapolating past performances, and/or c) going with gut feelings. At least 2 out of the 3 are totally subjective and false (3 for 3 if you are any good at creative accounting).

Are there any types of targets that can screw things up for you? The management accounting system perhaps? Ever heard of balanced scorecards? Thought so.

Why do companies have targets? Why do we measure people all the time? The obvious reason is to condition people to do what we pay them to do: focus. The other reason is that a company has to hedge against poor line and middle management and must manage its respective employees from the top down. It must ensure that people are working somewhere between overly enthusiastic and in total despair, both of which drive risky behavior. The perfect employee is motivated by increasing responsibilities and is kept from becoming arrogant and lazy by hard–to-reach targets.

In terms of assessing the risk of targets, you are right in the middle of a perfect storm. Targets and target fulfillment in large companies will be one of the main inhibitors of breakaway success for your venture.

Here's one easy example. Your company is selling ice cream by the pound to supermarkets. Your sales guys get commission based on pounds sold per week. Your financial system and management accounting is set up to monitor weekly sales according to flavor. Your supply chain reads weekly sales reports and sends weekly orders to production.

Now you come up with the bright idea of launching the shish-kebab-flavored ice cream with a revenue share business model together with convenience stores.

You have set up a completely new supply chain. You have top management's approval, you have the agreements with the stores in place, and you have an existing sales staff ready to go.

But . . .

As you get going, your sales staff quickly loses interest, even though your sales are growing at a steady pace. The sales staff, working on commission, can sell huge amounts of vanilla ice cream to supermarkets for a small effort as opposed to putting in a large effort at convenience stores for a small amount of actual target fulfillment. And even though revenue share ice cream at convenience stores might be a much better net margin business, and clearly is the future, the sales staff has reason to stay away, and hence, your shish kebab ice cream venture will fail. No matter how much you scream and beg, they will, at best, make an effort one time and only when top management is observing.

Sound somewhat familiar? You bet. Being outside the target fulfillment loop by, for example, trying to push a contradicting business model into a large company is extremely risky. It can be done of course, but only with a fair amount of effort, and we will come back to this later. For now you just need to honestly assess where your venture will sit compared to your company's existing incentive and management accounting system.

Answer these 4 questions prudently without aspirational thinking:

1.   Is your proposed venture in-line with your company's existing **business model**? Meaning that it does not contradict sales or production methodologies (subscription instead of bulk sales, B2C instead of B2B) or financial and capitalization structures (financing instead of capital expense)? YES OR NO.

2.   Is your proposed venture in-line with the existing **payment structure** of your company? Will you be able to reuse existing settlement processes or will you need to invent something new such as pay per use instead of pay up front, installments instead of one time, accumulated usage instead of expected peak capacity etc? YES OR NO.

3.   Will your venture make the targets in senior management's **balanced scorecard** easier to reach? For example, will your new venture have a shorter payments due cycle or will your new product need your company to change its ways of working with customers? YES OR NO

4.   Will your new venture have a positive impact on current **incentive schemes** in your company (mainly valid for the sales functions)? For example, your company may offer an incentive scheme that rewards large one-time orders with lower margins or it may reward the sales people who sell software with high margins but at a low volume. YES OR NO

Remember your answers for later.

Chapter 9 - Resources

"Resources. What about them? I have several R&D sites to choose from, and everybody will want to work for me since my new venture will be cool. In addition, I am a good manager and a pretty nice person."

This section is not about you at all — it's about everybody else. This section is about tapping into the potential of your own organization, about aligning with strategic HR policies, and about understanding your HR environment. The importance of this cannot be understated.

Case in point: our new ice cream flavor. How many ice cream makers in the company know how to create this specific taste? How many sales guys have knowledge of this totally new channel and its very specific requirements? How many employees do you need to make your venture successful, and have you received headcount approval for the bare minimum?

In a nutshell this is what the resource dimension is all about. You can't do everything by yourself. Not even with a strong co-founder will you be able to pull off any great feats in a large company. As soon as you start selling internally, acquiring resources, and gaining customer traction, all questions will end up on your table. In addition, working in major corporations involves significant overhead, and you will have to take this into account when planning your resource requirements. Something that in a start-up would require 1 full-time employee will take at least 1.5 full-time equivalents in a larger company. This is because you simply can't focus on building your own business in isolation. You have to handle several layers of management too, and this is normally done by giving them status presentations and holding more meetings. Meaning more work.

In terms of actual risk, the main risk is not having enough people, or the right people for the task to help you build or sell your solution. It's not easy to employ the right folks. And without people, your business venture will remain forever a hobby. Every good person added to the team early on in the life cycle will exponentially increase speed and performance. Conversely, every rotten apple will spread its disease to everybody else in record time.

In larger companies, it is also not that easy to simply let people go. Once you have someone on your team, you are destined to have them for the foreseeable future; conversely, in a start-up you can fire people quickly and replace the rotten apples with fresh ones. This comes back to the notion of pivots, or rapid changes of direction (all the rage in most popular entrepreneurial model of the day). They are hard enough as-is in start-ups and basically impossible in large corporations.

You will find plenty of books on how to find the best person for the job but surprisingly few on how to quickly identify the pathologically moronic and destructive employees (come to think of it, this might be our next book. We only write out of frustration, by the way).

The assessment itself around the Resource Risks gravitate around how you want to staff your venture. This is key. No successful venture survives without a critical mass of employees upon launch.

1.   Are there enough **competent people at arm's length** within your company? I.e. will you have a reasonable chance at getting access to appropriate competence? YES OR NO.

2.   Are you generally allowed to **employ many people** in batches from the outside? YES OR NO.

3.   Can you give your potential recruits ample notification **9 months in advance of when you will really need them** (this is the standard lead time between job posting to person joining your team and reaching the minimum acceptable performance level)? YES OR NO.

4.   Have you received **headcount approval** to support your growth? YES OR NO.

Remember your answers for later.

Chapter 10 - Alignment

Do you feel aligned within your team? This is not an assessment question, but we had to ask and this is usually the first question that you should ask as well. More precisely, have you conveyed your opinion as often and in as many ways needed to make your team align with you? And by alignment we not only mean the mandatory nod of a head around the conference table, we also mean that all sitting around the conference table nodding truly understand what they are in for and support the idea wholeheartedly.

Alignment in larger companies means meetings. And a few more meetings. And a last meeting just to make sure. No wonder it takes time to reach decisions. And as the organizer, you will (or should) be calling the meetings.

What is the difference between alignment and persuasion? Beats us. Your task as the intrapreneur is to convince everyone under the sun that your project is the one and only, the chosen one. Align your way to their hearts and be top of mind. This is easier said than done. Most of your time will be spent selling your idea to your peers and partners. Ironically, in the customer-first corporate world, customer interactions on a broader scale come later.

What do you need to align then? "Everything" is the shortest possible answer. You should, however spend some extra time with the following:

1.   Strategy groups (technical and commercial),

2.   Sales teams (global, regional, local),

3.   Development organizations ("yours" and others), and

4.   The execs, who among themselves might not be very aligned at all, even though they are in the same leadership team.

The aforementioned teams are not only vital to your success, but also inherently risky to deal with — they will all have strongly opposing agendas, i.e., "I want to keep my job and promote myself at all costs." Additionally, these teams usually consist of highly opinionated and usually very influential people. Just imagine having the perfect pitch but forgetting about the needs of the corporate strategy group (who speaks to the CEO on a daily basis, you or them?).

Do you really think that the mid-level executive will dare to give you funding if they are not sure if the venture fits within the company's overall go-to-market strategy? The execs also want to keep their jobs, probably more desperately than you do. Where else will they get overpaid for sitting in meetings all day and screaming general purpose read-it-last-week-on-LinkedIn advice to their juniors?

Basically the main risk associated with alignment is not doing enough of it. But time is scarce, and you are not the only one with a packed agenda. And when do you know that you have aligned enough? First a disclaimer: your alignment activities will vary over time. Second, as with most things in life, expect diminishing returns if you overdo it. Our experience tells us that the old 80-20 rule is a good start. That is, 80 hours a week of alignment and 20 hours of sleep. No, not really. But you should spend 80 percent of your time selling your idea internally like there is no tomorrow. Or, selling as if there will be no more funding in a month's time. The latter will, in most cases, be very close to the truth.

"80 percent of my time? Are you kidding? I need to do some proper work, like emailing requirements . . ."

Doing work other than actually selling your venture ideas will lead to . . . drumroll . . . less selling of your venture ideas! You need your Net Promoter Score (person likely to recommend to others) to be high enough internally before you can sell anything at all to customers, i.e., real sales = money.

Risk When Aligning with Strategy Groups

You have a strategy group at your company, don't you? If your answer is "no", then you simply don't know your company well enough. Go find it!

Strategy teams are to corporate executives what the Oracle of Delphi was to the god Apollo. Oracles were a source of divine knowledge and predictors of the future. The oracles acted as advisors and comforters to the aristocracy, political leaders, and military commanders. Ring a bell? The oracles, who listened directly to what the gods had to say, were seen as more trustworthy than your commonplace seers, who simply interpreted signs in the way birds flew or flowers grew in a particular season, etc. You can see where this is going.

Here is a simple comparison of the Oracle of Delphi and our modern day oracles, our beloved management/strategy consultants:

	Strategy Consultant	Oracle of Delphi
Customer	Corporate, military, and political leaders	Corporate, military, and political leaders
Product	Advice and forecasts	Advice and prophesies
Source of insight	Analyst reports and intuition	Words of the gods and intuition
Main mode of presentation	Sitting or standing in front of a PowerPoint presentation drinking coffee, intoxicated by self-embrace and general narcissism	The Pythia (Oracle of Delphi) would, when about to deliver, chew leaves from Apollo's sacred laurel tree and would then sit on her holy tripod on top of a crack in the rock from where noxious volcanic fumes emanated
Payment	Money	All types of sacrifices
Impact on your everyday business and customers	None	None
Impact on individual corporate strategic decisions	Sadly, quite high	Ditto
Implementability of advice, say, a few levels below top management	The what of the what? We don't understand the question. We could, however, offer to do a project to gain some insights into your problems . . .	Still chewing leaves and inhaling toxic gasses . . .

Chart 2: Strategy Consultants vs. The Oracle of Delphi. Copyright 2013 - ThirdRisk®

Leaders always want to convey prophecies. In large companies especially, the leaders are trained and expected to be the visionaries and the know-it-alls of the business. However, since we already know that sometimes office politics can anoint the most moronic of people to management positions, this is often not the case. At best your run-of-the-mill manager is, well, average. And the best managers you ever had were probably average with a bit of additional luck in hand. These average managers — do you think that they are capable of producing hundreds of slides and pages of Word documents covering the next five-year strategy for their units?

Hell no. What do you think the management consultants feed off?

1. Office politics (i.e., managers can easily escape the firing squad by blaming the consultants who made the foul strategy in the first place).

2. Hubris (It's my shish kebab ice cream department, and that means I am the leader. I am God's gift to business execution. We need a well worked through strategy with lots of pages and lots of graphs, in bright colors, that I can show off and store in the root folder of our corporate data repository for everybody to see and admire. My personal shrine for coming generations, my own dent in the universe).

3. Stupidity (no comment needed).

You know what the irony of it all is? Many of the corporate strategy team members are outcast top/middle tier strategy consultants themselves. What happens when the large strategy firm wants to get rid of people who underperform and will never become top managers? They try to get them employed with their customers and give them vague promises: "You just need a couple of years of hard-core industry experience before you can come back and we make you partner, given, of course, that you give us lots of high-profile strategy assignments in your new role within our customer's corporate strategy team."

Conspiracy theory, you cry? OK, OK, there might be some other profiles working within the corporate strategy teams. Who might they be? Apart from offbeat and general persona-non-grata crowds of lifetime-corporate-serving zombie drones? Beats us.

The strategy team's bread and butter is in providing general high-level advice based on management consultant reports, or to call it as it is, reading fairytales and telling bedtime stories. This is all fine and well for you, since this will not in the slightest way affect your small venture. But here's where the danger lies: some executives actually listen and have confidence in the strategy group and will *gasp* ask for some real advice once in a while. Like: "What do you think of this guy and his new idea?"

The executive in this case is expecting a one-sentence answer from the strategy group, and this answer will serve as the single piece of information in their decision to fund your venture.

But where exactly is the definitive risk? For now, let's just say that you should not in any way obstruct the strategy team's predisposed view of the world. If you argue with the Oracle of Delphi, the gods will get angry and your ship will sink.

Strategic planning is a game of charades — everybody knows this, including top management. Nobody really believes the strategy group's projections. The purpose of the strategy group is to provide one extra layer of accountability between upper and middle management. If the strategy group recommends investment avoidance, upper management can simply hide behind the group's research and official report stating thus. If a strategy group actually recommends investment, the senior executives can agree in public yet drag their feet behind the scenes, secretly betting that by the time actual money needs to be invested and budgets redesigned, technology has changed and the market has shifted. A new report from the strategy group will be promptly ordered by upper management, resulting in little causality and virtually no radioactive fallout from their original investment decision. And the music keeps playing and the merry-go-round of corporate strategic "initiatives" keeps spinning. Nauseating isn't it?

Risk When Aligning with Sales Teams

ABC. "Always be closing," screamed Alec Baldwin at his tired and petrified sales rep audience in the 1992 film *Glengarry Glen Ross*.

Sure, you always want to be closing, but with the internal sales team. Closing with this team is the main element that you need to be focused on initially. And don't buy a single sales self-help book because if you do, it is already too late. Guess who will spot a phony pitch from miles away? Never try to bullshit a bullshitter, and top-end sales people are instinctual bullshitters. Your key counterpart (sales director) will have you for breakfast, lunch, and dinner and then send you the bill.

Having been in sales for so long, we would go as far as to say that many senior sales leaders will actually enjoy embarrassing you and your phony read-it-in-a-book sales pitch: "consultative selling," "only asking open-ended questions," "beating the buyer," etc. By all means, use these techniques, and good luck. And when we see you next, please use a clean rag on our windshield.

Generally speaking, what motivates sales people? Fame and fortune of course. Don't believe us? Next time you're speaking with one of your colleagues in sales, ask to see his cell phone background, or better yet, look at his Facebook profile picture. Chances are he either has a picture of a Ferrari (his own if he is good) or his girlfriend, provided she's extremely attractive, of course. Or maybe he's doing some sort of extreme sport, or giving the camera his best "Blue Steel" look. The sales guys want to show off success, or at least their smokescreen of success. The guy with a picture of someone else's Ferrari could, all other things equal, become the key guy for you. Get him excited about the possibilities of fast and humongous success and you will be best friends all the way to payday.

Your risk with the sales team is twofold:

1.   You can completely blow it if you don't get them excited, and;

2.   You can make a complete dork of yourself and not be welcomed back.

The best way to blow your pitch is to refer to the strategic importance of your product. "Strategically important product" is salesperson code for loss-leading-hard-to-sell-will-soon-be-killed-and-create-huge-perception-problems product. Do this and you are toast right away. Slightly different than dealing with the strategy group, huh? You bet.

Who knows how to bring customers' money into the company's account? Who knows what the customers are actually willing to pay for? The strategy consultants? ROTFLMAO (ask your teenage child or Google it).

Risk When Aligning with Development Organizations

Do you want to goof around making presentations all day and ultimately disappoint? Or do you want somebody to develop your product? Of course you want the latter. Developing an idea into a tangible product is the whole point. So who will do this? Divine intervention or the actual engineers in your company? Ask the Oracle of Delphi.

We bet you have very capable engineers, managers, directors, and product designers who will gladly meet with you to discuss your new venture. But will they immediately start working on your prototype? Nope.

"But they all agreed that this was the best-tasting ice cream since strawberry margarita, which we launched last year. They agreed that this year is THE year for shish kebab. Nobody is doing anything other than agreeing!"

This might be fine, to start. Getting your development team enthusiastic about your idea is great. However, if you want to get people to work for you, you need a few really important pieces of information.

First, development teams and development managers want to bet on the new idea that will be a going concern. Something that will not be liquidated within the foreseeable future (i.e. 12 months in business terms) is not enough. They want to see something that could last forever. If you do not have a product or solution that will become so deeply engrained into a specific development unit that it can basically never be moved to another unit, you will not get the development managers' love. Today's development managers know one very important thing: they know that engineering and development services are a commodity. There will always, always be someone else in the world fighting to take over their jobs, either offshore or on. Development managers are a cost center in the corporate accounting world. Zero profits are directly attributed to working 10 percent more efficiently in the development organization compared to the year before. Sure, the product manager who allocates the budget on a completely different level of abstraction might get some of the credit for raising margins. But the development unit won't.

Which brings us to the second reason why development units will not immediately jump on board with your new venture: you need to come with money — you need to travel on sales trips and be armed with riches. Remember what we said about development units being a cost center. That is, all the guys and girls working in them are paid for by some product manager somewhere. Which in turn means that anything done outside of "normal" work will be on somebody else's tab.

Maybe the product manager will be you in the future — which is, of course, the message you have to convey. You are the person with the perpetual concern that will secure the development manager her very own chiefdom for eons ahead. The development manager will be the Queen of Hearts and will be able to lifestyle-work her way to retirement by betting on you.

We know you don't have the money yet. That's the whole point of the book. But you can always thicken your wallet with embellishment a little bit, and it would help if you raised internal money before. Come armed with, at the very least, a smaller prototype budget to wave around.

Risk When Aligning with Senior Executives

Ah, finally you get to meet the execs for a full hour of undivided attention.

Dream on.

If you manage to book an hour-long meeting, you will get, at most, 5 to 7 minutes of attention. For the rest of the meeting, you will pitch to a smartphone or laptop with moving lips. Emails will get sent and read, and constructive talk will devolve into the latest tidbits of office gossip. Funny how that works.

The main risk here is not grabbing attention within the first 10 minutes, which means a 5-minute presentation, a 3-minute discussion, and 2 minutes to assign action points to people you need to take a closer look at your venture. Getting actions points from the top executive is your key to success. Set yourself up for it.

"But this isn't how it works. Our executives understand the importance of cross-functional revenue streams and investing in new areas of innovation."

Yes, on a philosophical and probably even on an intellectual level, they do understand that innovation needs to be fostered and entrepreneurialism should be promoted. But don't forget what we said earlier. These people are in the business of hedged bets and watered-down financial investments. At best they understand yet simply don't wish to put their department under the spotlight. At worst, the executives you are pitching to are either former sales guys or former strategy consultants. Enough said.

1.   Does your venture contain or appeal to any part of your **corporate strategy**? YES OR NO.

2.   Is your venture's product **sellable within the current calendar year**? Will you at the very least be able to book orders during the current fiscal year? YES OR NO.

3.   Have you raised internal **budgets** before or do you already have, for example, a substantial demo budget? YES OR NO.

4.   Is your calendar at least 80% filled with **alignment meetings** yet? YES OR NO.

Remember your answers for later.

Chapter 11 - Communication

W e bet:

1.   You're not doing enough of it.

2.   You're terrible at it.

Either of these will wreak havoc for you and your venture. Combined —
certain doom. Effective communication is hard, especially within teams
in large companies. There isn't a single manager who has ever been
accused of communicating too much. Most people probably feel that you
are either not communicating nearly enough, or worse, convoluting the
original message.

For the sake of this book, what we really care about is telling you how to
compile and bring your measurable communication strategy to the table.
You will always lose if you don't have a properly developed
communication plan.

Just some food for thought. The anthropological view of communication
is what you should embrace, and we take this for granted:
communication happens between at least two humans.

Email is not human communication, voicemail is not human communication, SMS is not human communication. You are, in all of these instances, communicating uni-directionally to a machine that cannot handle emotions and that filters out context. Proper communication is done between people and in person. Digital communication is fine (i.e., chat and video), and telephone is passable. But just don't expect people to have read, remembered, or understood something that you sent in an email a week ago.

Many companies still utilize internal communications departments. It is the role of this department to disseminate and actualize the watered-down messages from top management. Apparently the whole point of this type of outdated communication is to ensure that the almighty leadership team can show their underlings that they still exist and can produce short intranet article quotations along these lines:

- Our company stands strong and is, as always, putting the good health of employees and their families first. With this in mind, this year you will see slight reductions in certain benefits compared to the previous insurance periods.

- The company has been successful in leveraging key resources and capabilities and has proven that we can add value to our shareholders over an extended period of time.

- Our core values are reflected in the team-player attitude of a few diligent employees who spent the entire weekend finalizing our strategic directional document, in which we describe how to win more business in the area of shish kebab flavored ice cream.

- Our company provides the most comprehensive suite of solutions for the lean production of Six Sigma–enabled strategic Big Data Cloud applications that will help our customers leverage the paradigm shift in ice cream distribution.

Ugh.

You are not top management. And getting, say, the VP of Internal Communications excited about your project will, at best, be rewarded with an intranet article that nobody reads. None mentioned none forgotten, the saying goes. Once you see some product manager mentioned and quoted in an intranet article, you know his or her fate is sealed. This person most likely reached out in desperation to the communication department when sensing that his or her product was going south. Again, none mentioned, none forgotten.

We don't know what school of communication actually teaches the internal communications people their lingo. All we do know is that you need to stay away. We challenge you to find an internal communications department that measures what any normal consumer communications department is measured on, i.e., Net Promoter Score or Engagement Index. Likely, its status is close to that of a knitting club, and its success is measured by how many articles are published (how many blankets were knit) and how many people read the last CEO message online (how many knitters came to the last knitting meeting). Sold anything yet to anyone, dear internal communications people?

Nope.

A few key communication principles constitute the foundation of a good communications strategy for your venture, as well as a good risk assessment:

1. Engagement

2. Conversations

3. Trust

4. Facilitation

If you excel at all of these you will always win the day. Our guess, however, is that you don't. In fact, we bet that you've never really thought about the 4 principles in a formal context before. Let's drill down into each one of them in order to show that while slightly different, they cumulatively form the foundation upon which good internal communication is built.

Engagement

One time when President Kennedy visited a NASA site, he met a janitor in a corridor. The president asked the janitor, "And what is your job?" The janitor replied, "Mr. President, I'm helping to put a man on the moon."

OK, OK. It's a bit cheesy, we know. But still, you need your foot soldiers on board. You need your able-bodied sailors to sail your ship towards the direction that you want to go.

A UK study led by CHA PR involving approximately 1,000 employees working in larger companies, indicated that 32 percent of staff on a grass roots level get one email from top management per month. 1/3! And you expect these guys and gals to carry your corporate strategy flag and wave it throughout the office?

According to the study, what were the top 5 methods of communication?

1.   Team meetings (71%)

2.   Leader visits (71%)

3.   Employee conferences (69%)

4.   Letters to staff (53%)

5.   Video (48%)

Figures in brackets indicate the percentage of staff members who found the approach very or fairly motivating.

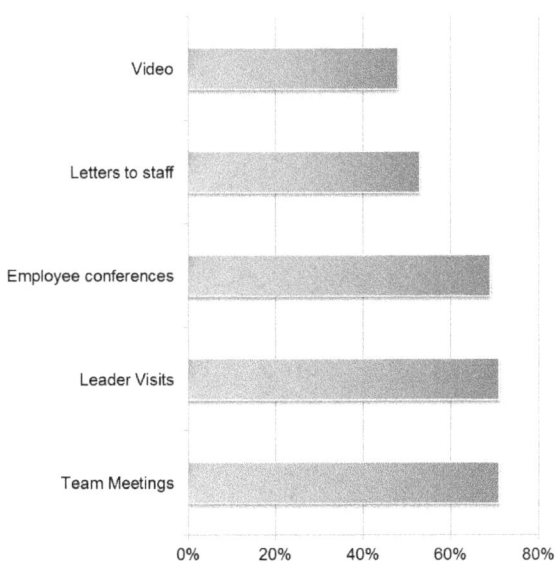

Chart 3: Employee engagement, top five methods of communication.

You can readily see from above what proved to be the most and least-effective communication channels. Staff meetings are by far the most effective and, according to the same study, the losers are newsletters and conference calls. Ever use teleconferencing to convey important messages? Think again. Apparently a grand total of 0 people think it is a good idea. The most important factor in gaining buy-in for just about anything within the corporate world is on-site physical presence. Meeting colleagues, shaking hands, sharing coffee — these simple gestures go so much farther in creating alignment than awkward teleconferences with 15 people and a 2 second latency delay. But we bet you've heard top management say that travel for internal meetings is prohibited due to cost. When travel restrictions and costs are being upheld for important internal meetings, the last gasps of entrepreneurialism within an organization can usually be heard. Next they will ask you to design your venture to be in line with the corporate strategy of "optimized opportunities", whatever the hell that means.

Conversations

As Winston Churchill said, "to jaw-jaw is always better to war-war." You now understand that you always need to immediately get people talking and engaging face to face. You might even ask some of the dopey senior managers to join. Now what? Shove another 45 minutes of death-by-PowerPoint presentation down their throats? Well, actually . . . yes.

"Say what?" We thought you were going to say something about Steve Jobs and never ever using PowerPoint for anything but dramatic pictures!"

Yes, we could have said that. And with good reason; allegedly Steve Jobs hated presentations.

But.

There is also a reason that rank-and-file executives love PowerPoint slides. The truth is that the audience members, regardless of title and size of office, more often than not actually don't know that much and are not as smart as they try to seem. The PowerPoint presentation acts as a comforter, or perhaps a pacifier, for both presenters and audiences alike. The gap between tacit knowledge and new ideas is neatly bridged by the slides themselves.

As you will inevitably be asked to send the slides to the execs after a meeting, always make sure that they are self-explanatory. Skip the fancy picture-only slides and shove in as much text as you can without it being impossible to read. Then all of the nodding heads in the presentation can go back to their darkened corner offices and actually re-read the content over and over again.

But what about the actual conversations?

Yeah. This was just the buildup.

During the main mode of conversation, your back will face a presentation screen. This somewhat hostile environment of presenter-facing-inattentive-audience is too common. Even worse, you might find yourself either in a cavernous meeting room or a hot and tiny hovel — the exact opposite to how most human beings would prefer as a setting for meaningful conversation.

How do you prefer to interact with friends and family? Do words such as "interactive," "inclusive," "intimate," and "interesting" resonate? Do these words in any way describe the content and setting that you are working with? Of course not. And therein lies an element of risk.

Face it, you are working with a venture that, at best, the execs will pay lip service to: "interesting," or "um, a very important area to investigate further later."

You will have to do better than that. You have to adapt quickly and be prepared. Make sure you appeal to the fact that we are working in a knowledge-based economy. Besides making money, many people actually enjoy learning new stuff. So if you don't know how to get ahold of some really good insight slides that relate to your industry, make sure to ask around and find out from where these can be sourced. This is by far the quickest way to gain attention and credibility during your presentation. And the quickest way to get a conversation going.

Be certain that if you end up at the coffee machine with THE executive sponsor you need, you're armed with a few good conversational topics that will lead you to getting a meeting. Regurgitate the latest *Financial Times* headline or even talk about the terrible coffee — say anything to get the opening. Just don't lose the moment.

Trust

This is a given, right? You have to be the Yoda of your venture. You have to be the person who people will trust and support, all the way through.

But. (Again.)

Large organizations are, at their core, highly cynical and untrustworthy creatures. And the people working in them, especially top management, are highly suspicious and paranoid.

Very few top managers would allow employees to run around and talk to other managers without controlling, for example, the presentation structure first. Your challenge is to come across as consistent and trustworthy. And this is where it gets rough.

"It takes a crook to know one." You will not appear trustworthy if you make statements to internal stakeholders such as "this solution provides increased shareholder value," or "this service will make our company a thought leader in the area of ice cream distribution." This is useless corporate-lingo diarrhea and always, always comes across as phony. Nobody genuinely gives a horse's ass about these statements, since 9 times out of 10, they will not end up in the target fulfillment specification. Furthermore, all of the other senior executives know that you made these statements to hide something less delightful about your venture. Maybe you are actually building another sheikdom in disguise and trying to eat their lunch. Come to think of it, you were sitting a little too close to the CEO at the recent company picnic . . .

See where this is going?

Your motives for asking someone to support your venture must be transparent and honest. That's the simple truth. If you are building the Tower of Babel, you need to create mutual understanding among your peers. Or else you will fail.

Facilitation

After seeing your 45 minute presentation deck and meeting you at the coffee machine, can anybody recite your venture's pitch? Absolutely, provided you were any good at all. And if you were decent, people will talk about your idea when you are not around. People will want to understand your idea. If you do not provide the means for doing so, people will just make things up according to their own belief systems.

There is a very high risk that your message will go through a game of telephone, where one person whispers in the ear of the next and the original message becomes distorted along the way.

What you need to do is create a network of ambassadors who can, with a few sentences, describe your venture without distortion.

"Easy-peasy! This is by far the most commonsensical piece of BS so far. Next please."

Hang on. What does making people "ambassadors" actually really mean?

For us, it comes down to a couple of simple principles:

- Don't be arrogant. Don't be the know-it-all. Yeah, we know you have all the answers. We know that people don't understand basic facts about life in general and that you have to correct them. But this will alienate your audience and make people insecure. Would you fight for someone else's idea if you felt insecure?

- Make people smart(-er). Are you truly trying your best to simplify? Remember the Star Trek metaphor? Maybe there are already easily accessible examples that you can use as a foundation. There is a reason that in the entrepreneurial world you often see statements like "we are the Facebook for dogs," or "we are the Nespresso for ice cream". They both address a technical, commercial, and business-model analogy at a very high level of abstraction. It works because people can relate. Don't overcomplicate and don't overestimate the novelty of your venture and/or invention.

Now, your final assessment questions:

1. If somebody screamed STOP after **3 minutes of your presentation**, would your audience know what you want to build and sell and to whom? YES OR NO

2. Do you run live **person to person** team meetings and employee conferences at a minimum of a bi-weekly basis? YES OR NO

3. Is your presentation deck **self-explanatory** when sent out after the meeting? Will people understand it when reading alone? YES OR NO

4. Will people **learn something** by listening to your pitch? YES OR NO

Now add up the number of times you answered "yes" to the questions posed throughout the book — maximum 16. Now divide by 4 to get the average. This is your ThirdRisk® score, and you will use it to create a winning strategy. Remember it.

Some notes on the questionnaire. The questions represent the majority of all the cases we have worked on and are generally applicable, but there are always corner cases. There is also a fair amount of subjectivity involved. Ask yourself "Really?" at least 3 times and try to answer prudently. There are many ways to ensure objectivity, such as peer review. Our patent pending (not really) 3 "Reallys," closely related to the 5 "Whys". By now you should understand that you can create your own 3-strikes-and-then-out-acting-like-a-pro investment analysis — just handle with care! By the way, do you still have the same score after circling back and checking your original answers?

Chapter 12 - Perspectives On Your Score

Before we dig deeper into the inner workings of the ThirdRisk® model, let's analyze what we have done so far and see what we can use this score for.

The score was generated based on your assessment of your venture's fit with the current operational and business model of your company. This is important because the lower your score, the less likely you will be able to, right off the bat, succeed on your intrapreneurial path. Again, the higher you score, the easier it becomes to succeed.

Why?

Because you are setting out on a course to find new routes to blue oceans, á la our friend Tolliver. Similarly, if you scored very low, your venture will need to change in order to be better aligned, or your company has to change in order for you to succeed. Either or. It's that simple, according to our model.

"Are you guys for real? Where did the entrepreneurial spirit go? Be more like entrepreneurs, break rules, fight bureaucracy!"

Sorry, we warned you that we might make you grumpy. But as we said, the model is weather-tested — it works more often than not. And, again, we apologize for being a little rough on all you bluest-ocean-entrepreneurial-management-book authors, but the ThirdRisk® framework allows you to be honest with yourself about what you need to do to be successful. It is, sadly, not as simple as just finding large underserved markets to address with a shiny new technology. In larger companies, you must also add the wet blanket of ThirdRisk®.

There are ways, however, to convince your patrons that the new-found land of opportunity will be more valuable than discovering the route to blue oceans. If you achieve a final score of 0 i.e. no questions answered with yes, you can still pull it off — it will just be a bit harder, and you will have to be a bit more elaborate in your steps.

Let's return to a modified version of our original chart. The numbers in the quadrants display the minimum ThirdRisk® score you need in order to successfully pass through (chart 5).

Pass through?

Yes, we will add the dimension of time and create a road map of your entrepreneurial journey through the 4 quadrants of the model. Think of it as navigating from point A in the bottom left corner to your state of Utopia in the upper right corner. Since this can only be done in sequences we add the dimension of time and instead of calling it turn-by-turn navigation we simply call it your venture's strategy. Your strategy on how to successfully mitigate and battle the ThirdRisk® head-on.

Let's put the score into another context. It's important that we are all on the same page here.

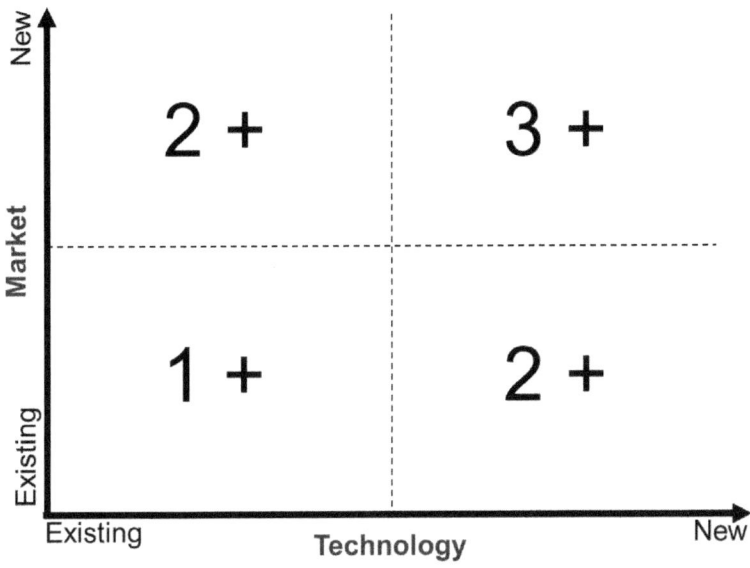

Chart 4: ThirdRisk scoring chart. Copyright 2013 - ThirdRisk®

Your score is not determined by Market Risk or Technology Risk. These risks are covered in your Opportunity and Feasibility Analysis. Your ThirdRisk® score will determine how likely you are to succeed within your current *political* settings. It shows you what you need to work on and how high your score should be, depending on how far your venture is pushing the limits of your company. The closer you are to your existing market and technology, the less politically challenging the venture will be and the lower your score can be.

Political minefields usually don't exist within smaller incremental development efforts. You can fly under the radar within smaller markets and with less complicated technological developments. But as soon as you set sail for India by way of the western route as opposed to the normal eastern route, you will sooner or later reach a point of no return and will inevitably accumulate enough political tension to set you off course.

"But, I want to change my company's operational model, and build a new Facebook — for cats!"

That's fine. But you will not be successful until you either adapt your plan to achieve a ThirdRisk® score of **2** or higher. This is because it is a new market and you will inevitably need to elevate out of your initial lower left quadrant or manage to work through the required pieces of the ThirdRisk® model within your company so that the operational model, business model, organization etc. fits with your new venture. The ThirdRisk® model basically says that the farther out you come in the outlandish scoping of either technology or market development, the higher ThirdRisk® score you will need to succeed.

It goes without saying that you will not be able to turn things around immediately, even if you do now recognize your increased chances for a risk of failure. Instead you will have to create a plan to get to where you want to be. And you need to keep at it for some time. It's a marathon not a sprint. You are navigating the blue ocean, remember, not the Central Park Duck Pond. It's not as easy as the entrepreneurial superstars in Silicon Valley might make it seem.

One last time: the farther out on the axis you are, the higher your score in the ThirdRisk® model needs to be if you want to succeed. The lower your score is the higher your risk will be. A low score is never good. A low score will make you weak.

"How can you be so sure it works? The ThirdRisk®, that is?"

We argue that all companies operate within a 3 dimensional system of risk. The first 2 dimensions are the market and the underlying technology used to serve the market need. This is the matrix within which all businesses, large or small, operate. These 2 dimensions have been heavily documented and preached thus far, are far easier to analyze in an objective manner. The 3rd dimension, involving much softer and less tangible qualities, is far harder to quantify.

All investments in a corporation, no matter the size, will be analyzed according to the dimensions of Market and Technical risk. Every single dollar of profit that is reinvested in the company, as opposed to being returned to the owners will be judged on its merits of created value. Anyone who chooses to subsequently reinvest back into the company are again putting those dollars at risk.

But what happened to the company between startup phase and current status? Successful initial growth of the company is a result of making the right and sometimes lucky decisions on Market and Technology risks. This has meant that the company has customers and has been rewarded with the possibility to employ more people.

And this lends to the core of our argument. What happened along the way is that people, not simply spreadsheets and academic frameworks, got involved. Effectively managing real people in real situations, with all of their discrepancies, perceptions, and quirks, is what this book is all about.

While the recruiting industry seems to imply via their algorithms and personality tests that all professional profiles are created equal and can be siloed, this is obviously not the case. No matter how regimented and compliant the internal work processes are, employees will still execute tasks with a degree of flexibility and discretion, and in what they believe to be the best way possible.

Dreams of being able to control human beings with modern one-size-fits-all-command-control-incentivize-systems will never completely be successful. The attempt to do so will create what at best will be called the "corporate culture", and at worst, antagonism. All companies have it and it will never go away.

The ThirdRisk® is all about the 3rd dimension. The ThirdRisk® needs to be taken into account and handled with as much care as the more tangible Market and Technology Risks. This framework is by no means the first publication to talk about the inner workings of large companies. But, as stated earlier, ThirdRisk® is the context of contexts, the aggregate of the underlying sentiments that drive your business, and what dictates what your execs can rubber stamp. We use this framework daily on ourselves and people we advise, and it works. Our foundation is our experience

Not convinced yet? Let's try to fill in the blanks with a case study to prove our point that nothing new ever gets invented and successfully brought to market without a successful ThirdRisk® score.

Chapter 13 - The Toyota Case

As a good example of what would seem to be an almost purely technology centric intrapreneurial venture, think of a car company like Toyota. Some smart and entrepreneurial mind at Toyota many years ago saw that the petrol combustion engine was in for a severe challenge. The angst was that legislation and consumer demand would continue to dictate that more fuel-efficient solutions must be provided. California was in the driver's seat in terms of lowering transportation emissions.

This bright Toyota engineer (it must have been an engineer, as we will soon see) also noted that most cars in major metropolitan settings are driven slowly for relatively short amounts of time with many starts and stops, which means a lot of wasted gasoline.

At the same time, drivers also wanted to make longer excursions at will with their families during the weekends and they did not want to sacrifice agility, comfort and utility.

Voila — the hybrid battery/combustion vehicle was born. The smart engineers at Toyota understood that combining the electric drive with a combustion engine would create a potentially disruptive technology. But even more importantly, they also understood that consumer demand for reliable, affordable, and versatile vehicles was so powerful that they could not simply develop something half-heartedly in order to test the market. They had to take the technology to a very high level of maturity before actually releasing it to the general public.

So, as the hybrid vehicle intrapreneur at Toyota, you would have to make a perfectly horizontal journey from the lower left corner of the ThirdRisk® model towards the very far right. You would, as Toyota always does, have perfected the technology in absurdum before ever releasing it to the market. The overall market was an existing market — the small-sized personal vehicle segment — and the sales channel was also already in place via their strong consumer brand recognition.

Toyota did not cannibalize existing sales much; instead, it advertised and appealed to additional segments of car buyers, thereby shifting slightly vertically in the ThirdRisk® model. The hybrid technology has, over time, found its way to an increasing number of Toyota and Lexus models (markets or segments, if you wish) and is now very close to being in the upper right corner of our model — the "Utopia" corner.

This was an entrepreneurial venture within a large organization that most likely had many political opponents and faced many alignment and communication hurdles. Arguably the hybrid drive initiative had a lot of things going for it, such as governmental and ecological economic mandates, as well as the fact that it was still actually a car (according to our model and probably all other models, a hybrid helicopter would most likely have failed on the drawing board).

Yet still Toyota invested huge amounts of money in a commercially and technically unproven technology during the course of several business cycles. Many technology-only initiatives fail before actually releasing anything to the market. The communication, alignment, and resource dimensions of the ThirdRisk® model inside Toyota must have been extremely powerful in securing top management's attention and willingness to invest.

Toyota undoubtedly had plenty of other ways to maximize fuel efficiency but chose to bet on a very risky technology that would most likely have been avoided by anyone who asked for advice from the major Management Consultant houses in the US (hello GM). Ironically, in the land of free commercialism, GM required government intervention before it finally released its disruptor — the Volt electric car.

For the sake of argument, in hindsight, Toyota might have benefitted from betting on more than one fuel-saving technology. It could also arguably be seen as late to the market with, for example, small turbocharged engines or extremely fuel-efficient diesel engines. But within the context of this book, you should instead notice how a powerful intrapreneurial venture executed in the right way can convince a large organization to remain steadfast on an unproven technology. Impressive to say the least.

What about the corner cases, the cases that fall outside of perfect boundaries? Toyota has been analyzed to death and has proven to be hard to replicate, we know.

The case is a very illustrative example of a technology initiative in wait of a market. A very long wait as it turned out. This is not the norm.

Actually, it is probably the most risky way to develop any new venture. Getting far out on a technology tangent before actually vetting it with the mass market is very, very hard to pull off. Instead the mantra of the day is to develop ever-so-little technology and then search for your market. Especially within the digital economies, such as consumer Internet. The high priests of Silicon Valley mumble mantras of lean start-ups, customer development, and iterating and pivoting. In short, methods for running technology start-ups with as little waste as possible while finding out if someone wants to pay, or use for that matter, your new photo-sharing app.

The pivot mechanism of Silicon Valley works like this: If nobody wants to share photos with your app, you turn it into an enterprise collaboration solution. When this also does not work, lastly, you turn into to a bunch of smart people searching for jobs (popularly referred to as "Aquihires," e.g., Facebook hiring people by buying your failing start-up). Which, by the way will also show up as a successful exit on the VC's portfolio web page. Worth considering when looking closer into the success rate of certain VC's.

But, this is not for you. By all means, listen to the talks, read the books, and fantasize about becoming rich and famous in Silicon Valley. Day dream of being the poster child of the VCs and best buddies with Sergey, Marissa, and Mark. But again, this is not for you. You need to play a totally different game. You are in the corporate world, where pivots are a function in Excel, where iterating, at best, means that your development team has adopted agile as a methodology. At worst, "iterating" refers to the way you make decisions. The corner case of the ThirdRisk® model is your everyday life. Launching a new electrical toothbrush based on a pulsating technology as opposed to oscillating technology is not very groundbreaking, even though you as the product manager might believe so. You also cannot simply launch a prototype and then listen to feedback and iteratively improve. What type of feedback do you think the first customers will have? What do you think your corporate lawyers will say about people putting prototypes in their mouths?

Instead, you will have to find a way to navigate the blue oceans of innovation in a way that will be executable and credible in your setting. We agree that most ventures in large companies are over-engineered and would benefit from being launched earlier and with a more limited feature set. This is especially true if you want to go after new customer segments once your product has reached saturation in your "home" market.

Chapter 14 - Charting Your Way to Utopia

So with the navigation and corner cases in mind, let's find your starting point on your journey to Utopia (the upper right corner). Navigation will begin, 99.9 percent of the time, somewhere in the lower left quadrant. Or at least it should if you have an existing technology addressing an existing market. You, the intrapreneur, are now thinking about ways to commercialize the same in a different way or proposing to develop new technology, i.e., move along either of the axes. If not, you have picked up this book very late in the process and really need to start working — hard.

Next, determine your end destination (somewhere in the envisioned future). Normally you would want it to be, if not all the way in the upper right corner, somewhere far along each of the axes with a final perpendicular turn. This will display your development of a new market or a new technology. We did ask you to consider this during your Opportunity and Feasibility Analysis phase, right? Now this actually becomes useful. Big idea: you primarily develop either a new market or a new technology to start with, never both at the same time (unless you often win the lottery, that is).

Your road to glory will later, for the sake of strategizing, need to be further dissected into manageable time frames and waypoints. Your final destination is mostly aspirational and will, in reality, very seldom be reached. Still, as they say, reach for the stars.

We will save the strategizing and practical advice for a later chapter.

An example of your path to Utopia. The round circles with numbers illustrate your plan for the coming three years, or eons, if that fits better with your company.

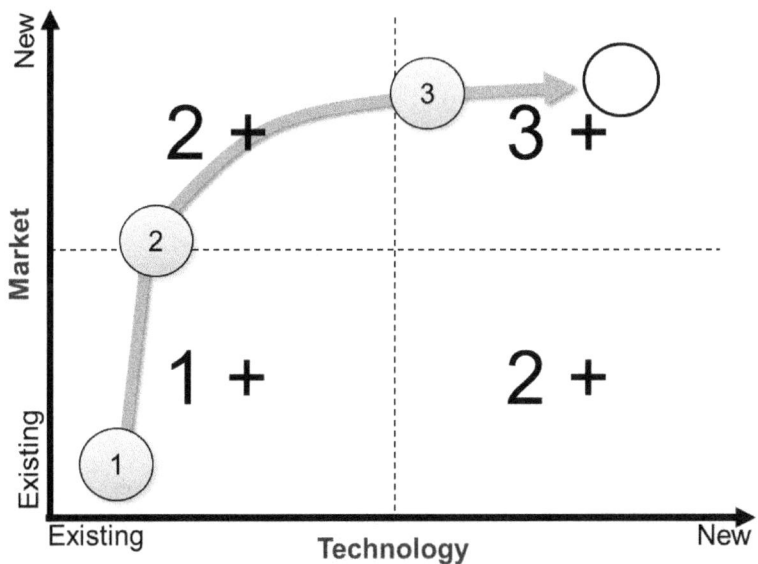

Chart 5: Charting your path to Utopia. Copyright 2013 - ThirdRisk®

What would Toyota's journey have looked like? First, it had a very long development path. The technology was completely new, but the initial market was the existing one. It launched and then later turned to other markets. The ThirdRisk® would have indicated that for quite some time, research and development could keep a low profile, with small teams and privacy controls. After roughly two decades of this type of obscure activity, a very strong intrapreneur saw merit and practical applications for this technology and secured increased funding for the project. This is when Toyota entered the 2+ ThirdRisk® territory. To emphasize how strongly the intrapreneur had to fight and manage the ThirdRisk®, the same development manager later went on to become the CEO of the whole company, partly because of the success of the hybrid technology products, such as the Prius, but also because he was a master at managing office politics.

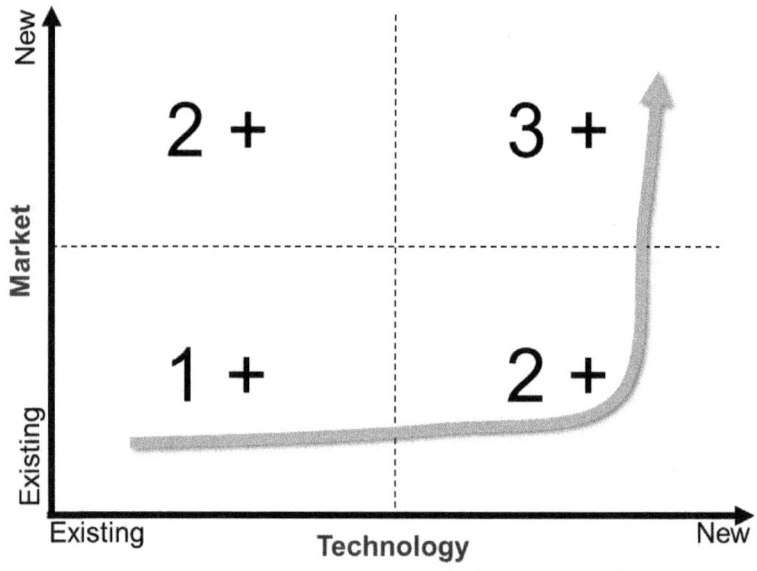

Chart 6: Toyota's path to Utopia. Copyright 2013 - ThirdRisk®

So, the ThirdRisk® quadrants are explained. Isn't there something else? Right! The Doldrums. The place where most intrapreneurs fail and where most projects are killed — the place where all the wind dies out and your crew stages a mutiny.

Anyone familiar with larger-scale sea navigation knows that many a historic sailing ship lost its way in this no-wind territory around the equator. Brave and/or ignorant captains constantly challenged the Doldrums. Very often these unsuccessful captains were either overconfident in both their crew and ship's abilities, or thought that they had found a shortcut via unsubstantiated theories of the undiscovered new wind belt.

In the same way, many intrapreneurs willingly believe plain market research and set sail for the next new thing without doing their own market research. This is a bad way to start your voyage. Would you start your dream vacation without ever checking out past guest reviews or travel tips for the area? You cannot, without assuming the possibility for almost certain failure, navigate the 2-by-2 quadrants in a straight diagonal direction.. Attempts to do so ensure that the idea will be destined for no-man's-land; i.e. the Doldrums.

Even worse, displays of hubris and pride by some will drive them to ignore any type of research at all, relying mainly on seemingly unsurmountable levels of funding capital. If you as an intrapreneur get too much funding (most often a consequence of unrealistic market projections) you will, without exception, set out on a mission to spend it. You have to, right? This is your chance!

Be very careful here. First of all, you must meet your revenue targets early on. This can lead you to either 1) target new markets too early or 2) branch out your product too early (over scoping features, over engineering technical solutions or simply create too many products for your organization to handle, etc.). Both instances will take your ship headfirst into the Doldrums.

Due to your giant pile of cash or the giant organization that you have created, you will have many prying eyes on you, a disproportionate amount of interest, a Frankenstein's Monster. You will end up with several managers and will ultimately have to surrender your own development beliefs to the hoard of small generals you helped to employ. Each of these generals will expect to be heard and recognized for each of their respective experiences and opinions. You are in danger of creating a bureaucracy within a bureaucracy, and you are destined for failure.

Management will undoubtedly ask you how many new markets you have opened up with your new pile of money. Or they might ask you how many of the new features you have sold. Or both. Your answer will always be disappointing. Especially since the frequency of the questions from your financiers and backers will increase over time. Even though top management has the intellectual ability to comprehend that, for example, entering new markets takes time, they also have higher-ups to report to. And when the chips fall, who will get the blame? Them or you? You will be toast and will be replaced by the "turnaround" guy who knows how to focus and won't mismanage funds. At the very least you need to hedge against management disappointment by displaying your prudent cost-management skills.

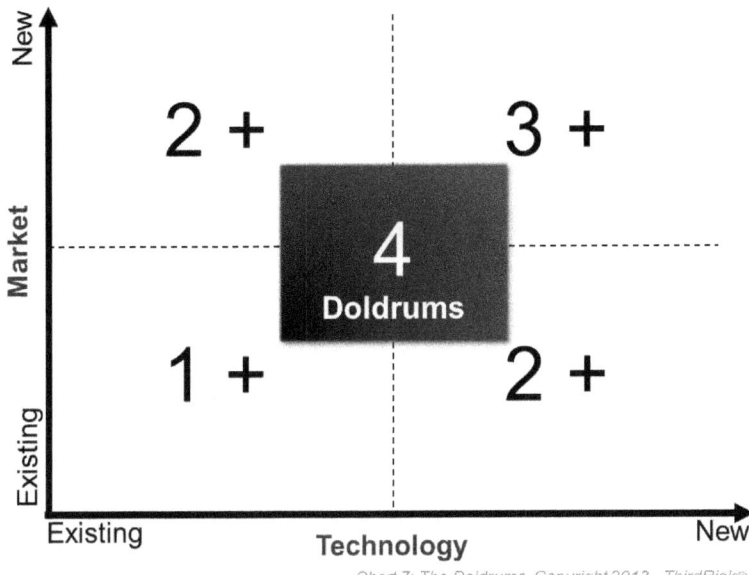

Chart 7: The Doldrums. Copyright 2013 - ThirdRisk®

The Doldrums of the ThirdRisk® model are best described with a case: the case of the high-tech innovators.

Chapter 15 - The High-Tech Innovators' Case

In the years after the dot-com crash, one of the major telecommunication vendors that was hit very hard by the crisis decided to venture out into the world of mobile payments. At the time, the most pressing need was enabling consumers to download ringtones, music files, and wallpapers to their mobile devices and pay for these products easily.

The solution was to connect mobile operators such as AT&T and Vodafone to a simple payment interface, which the external application providers could use for small transactions that ultimately ended up on the subscriber's bill. The idea itself was not totally new in the market, and the fundamental technology existed within arm's length of the telecommunication vendor's own organization. What was not in place, however, was the operational model, organization, finance/management control system, and support for the business model, which would involve feeding off a revenue share of millions of small transactions (the vendor's normal business model was selling large infrastructure projects).

So the intrapreneurs (there were two founders) had an existing technology for a totally new market. Hence, their tangent was directly vertical — they only had to adapt existing technology to fit their needs. So far so good. Now what? How can we use the ThirdRisk® model to a) assess the likelihood of them succeeding and b) on the flip side of things, create a strategy for them to mitigate potential ThirdRisk® shortcomings?

Our high-tech intrapreneurs within the telecommunications vendor had an initial score of **1.9**. They scored high on communication and resources but low on targets and alignment. They were also clearly heading in the direction of market development in the upper left corner and needed a higher score. So what should they do, according to the ThirdRisk® model? Here comes a key piece of advice: even though it is not always needed, balance between the dimensions is always better. If you score disproportionately low in one area, you will have a much steeper hill to climb when the going gets tough — and it will. The high-tech intrapreneurs intuitively worked within the ThirdRisk® model and understood that they needed to work on alignment first. They did, however, misjudge the effort they needed to put into targets, as we will see later.

Just shy of one year down the road, the technology, organization, and product was ready to launch. The year had been spent on selling, installing technology, and building a basic organization. They also decided to circumvent the targets dimension altogether by spinning the whole venture into a separate legal entity with a separate financial system. Upon launch, the new unit was a breakaway success in terms of increasing number of customers, transactions, and revenues. Everybody was happy, right?

Wrong.

Two years down the line, unease developed within the management team. The patrons in the mother ship were starting to become increasingly "interested" in how this new unit was being run. Every week there were more and more directional steering meetings, and the faces of the two founders were becoming more and more disgruntled. What happened?

Two main things, in fact. First, the company was seen as very opaque. The decision to work around, instead of with, the existing management control and finance systems was obviously in hindsight a poor idea. They lacked key stakeholder buy-in and this affected the product's long-term credibility. Second, the unit's intrapreneurs had requested, and been given, a huge amount of funding to broaden the portfolio and extend the technology about one year earlier. They, however, had failed to deliver on their promise of a rapid increase of new customers and revenue targets.. What was their ThirdRisk® score at this time? **2.9**.

This score should have allowed them to turn horizontally, to the right, and develop new markets — had they come far enough on the market development axis. What happened instead was that the organization was under severe pressure to do everything at once and was plagued with money to spend. Once you have it, you have to spend it or it will disappear.

Remember the Doldrums? That's where the intrapreneurs are now. They tried to do everything at once while trying to maintain a growing core business, which by the way, was not the self-playing piano it seemed to be. What happens according to the great oracle of ThirdRisk® once you get into the Doldrums?

1. You fail and shut down, or

2. You are fired and replaced by the turnaround expert, or

3. You have a ThirdRisk® score of a perfect **4** and manage to pull through.

Our friends, the high tech intrapreneurs, did not have a score of **4**. They could not fight against the micromanagement of their patrons and ultimately ended up leaving the company. What happened to the unit? A turnaround expert was brought in, the financial system was consolidated, and the focus shifted to the core business (i.e., the vertical ascent continued until it had enough business volume to break away, which didn't happen for another two years, when the unit launched its first adjacent product offering).

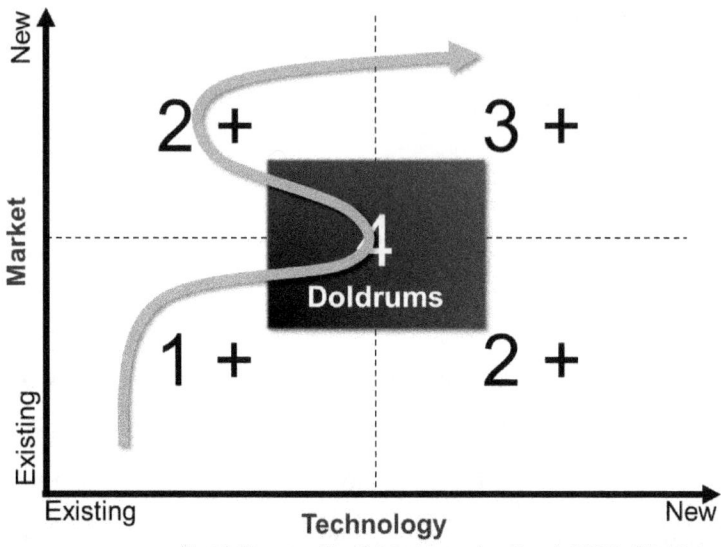

Chart 8: The case of the High-tech Innovators. Copyright 2013 - ThirdRisk®

Ultimately the unit was successful with a few core product offerings for quite some time, but the ThirdRisk® score never reached above **3.2**, and more importantly, the mother company never embraced the new business model on a wider scale. Once the market was eventually saturated, the unit was spun off in an executed exit scenario (e.g. selling or closing down) instead of invested in. In Venture Capital terms, this would have been a successful exit (1 out of ~10, remember?). Even though the business could have fared better for the investors, in this case the mother company, they did get a net positive return. However, a stronger ThirdRisk® score would have given the unit a better chance of preparing for the future at an earlier stage by, for example, allowing for more freedom to go after new markets (senior management in the mother company prevented this). This in turn would most likely resulted in a greater return on investment during the entire business cycle as well as in the exit scenario.

PART FOUR

Your Game Plan

Though we understand that all businesses and industries have unique characteristics, we also know that ultimately, people are quite similar no matter where they work or where they come from. Obviously the notion of workplace conformity clashes with the popular mantra of diversity and individualism, but the somewhat boring truth remains that most business decisions and corporate fallacies follow a very similar pattern. Maybe we should blame it on Anglo-Saxon schooling, business principles and colonialism? Or is it due to our global interconnectedness and the fact that we all gossip about our respective office politics via Facebook?

In actuality, we don't really care. Being too mindful of, and adaptable to, local conditions, and trying to analyze each stakeholder's personal management style and personality traits in an attempt to mitigate all project risks and caveats will not lead you anywhere. You will either spend far too much time preparing and analyzing or will alienate far too many people in your attempt to take all needs and wants into account.

So, in a few sentences, we have annulled the tens of thousands of books and articles on behavioral and adaptive leadership. By all means, read all of them and come to your own conclusions. But our experience tells us that the insights and "practical" tips you get from these theories involve twisting yourself into a tangled mess. Trying to accommodate everything ensures that your message will become diluted, weak, and useless.

In the following chapters we will take you through the 4 steps needed in order to achieve a higher ThirdRisk® score. The order of the steps might not fit you perfectly, but try and view the steps as a way to structure and sequence your thinking in a way that we have always found to be a helpful.

Chapter 16 - Step 1: Strategic HR

"HR Management" has been a central concept in an increasingly intensified focus on rebranding the Human Resource department. Rebranding efforts are trying to take HR away from being viewed as a plain resource management organization, towards having a much more strategic influence on the company's success. Comparing a living, breathing "resource" with, say, a pallet of paint cans is a somewhat unnerving exercise. And while the corporate world has definitely gotten better at defining and refining the role of HR departments, to many it still remains slightly fluffy. On top of all of its formal responsibilities, the HR department is still the dumping ground for a lot of the softer issues an organization faces. As a result, it often gets overlooked when new and exciting ideas and business models are proposed.

Truthfully "HR" sounds a bit 1980s to our ears. Yes, the increasingly common term is "Human *Capital* Management," but the new terminology does little to bring the actual concept into the 21st century. Today it seems that advanced HR departments should be called "staffing strategy departments" or maybe "headcount fanatics."

Request some more headcount with a decent rationalization and you actually might get them. But where do these people come from? Are they pulled from different departments, or are they new hires? Nobody outside of the senior members of the HR department, no matter how high up on the food chain they might actually be, seems to really know where the increased headcount comes from. It has been whispered at water coolers and slurred at corporate retreats that headcount allocation is a convoluted corporate process most likely invented by the HR departments themselves to create leverage and increase job security. And while we are unsure about exactly why the formalized concept of HR was created, we do know that when requesting a significant change in overall headcount numbers, HR needs to be directly involved. HR holds the secret formula regarding personnel reassignments.

To be honest, we would not be surprised if even the top managers at large companies don't exactly understand the implications of headcount allocation. This is readily apparent when steering meetings are held to discuss the topic. Most likely the following scenario will occur:

SCM (Steering Committee Meeting) Chair: "OK, we are doing all right this year. It looks like we are potentially redlining the utilization levels of our available project personnel. We should increase headcount."

The rest of the SCM nods and murmurs approval.

SCM Chair: "OK, good. Let's say we increase headcount by 5 percent over the coming year. HR lady in the corner, what's your name again?" [It always seems to be a woman, by the way.]

Without allowing her to respond, the chair continues in rapid-fire style.

"Create a program to increase our headcount by 5 percent. Do the usual stuff — recruit at universities, steal a few from suppliers and customers. How should we distribute these new additions? Well, do what we always do. Require managers to create extended business plans for their respective units. We, of course, will not read these plans but it will weed out the least motivated who only come with a 20-page plan. Then we will scatter the headcount at will — their plans will never play out anyway. And lastly, don't forget to require managers who get a lot of increase to also fire a few low performers to send a message."

Sounds unrealistic and exaggerated? Wait until you get to that level, and then please remember this part of the book. At least you'll have a private laugh.

The people who really run the company are the hordes below which diligently execute and create processes. The personnel game is born within the ranks of middle management. And guess who helps middle management with the people thing? Yep — HR.

HR is not there to secure the best situation for all employees. HR is there to support and guide middle management through the yearly headcount game. That's it. SO USE THIS TO YOUR ADVANTAGE. Don't sob about all those times you confided your deepest career aspirations to HR in the hope of scoring that top position. HR people are not your high school guidance counselors. This is also not the time to mourn the lost opportunity you might have created as a result of all those times you treated that HR employee like an administrative assistant.

First, remember that most HR "assistants" have advanced degrees and also understand a thing or two about strategy and finance, especially since they are part of a wide variety of strategic decision meetings. Don't mix HR up with, for example, marketing folks, who by in large have no real clue (but should) of what you really want to achieve with a new venture. In fact, spend as little time as possible with the marketing department when promoting your new venture, as it will most likely lead to nothing.

Instead, invest your time with the HR people. Make sure you are always in the back of their minds when headcount musical chairs is being played every quarter/year/series. Make sure you land that intern (free resources), make sure you are the first person HR turns to when the high-potential-program employees need placement, and make sure you can give your employees the credit they deserve (HR can help you find incentive systems outside of the normal ones).

All of this might sound counterintuitive to many seasoned intrapreneurs. We also understand how silly it might seem that HR, the people you normally stay away from when trying to solve business problems, actually can help you out with your venture. But truly above all else, a strong relationship with the HR department can help you solve impending political problems.

HR has a view of the organization that you never will, and it is one of very few organizational units that can easily navigate around normal office politics since it sails under the "softer" flag of "corporate values," "mission statements," and the "greater good." No manager in any corporation wants to be the person who, in front of senior HR executives who in turn will be part of his next performance review meeting, imply things such as "your idea will make my organization irrelevant and potentially save the company lots of money". In front of HR all managers with half a brain know that you have preach the high gospel of greater good and at the very least make an effort to pretend that you actually care about other things than your own salary increases and growing your own kingdom. You get it, right?

Practically speaking then, as the intrapreneur designing a new venture, what are the key things you should discuss with HR?

First: make sure you can answer the first question in the deck:

HR: If we approve this, what are the implications on the rest of the organization's personnel count and how do you intend to secure a resource increase?

Second, you have to put your imagination to work and tried to create a scenario where somebody (a manager) in the company has a similar proposition. Is there a chance that this person would try to backstab you? Is there a chance that somebody could try to discredit you and your idea in order to save face and protect his or her existing fiefdom? If you have the slightest hunch about a situation like this, you should bring it up in the HR session, however you must not whine and vent. You need to sell the idea first and then ask for advice on how to handle the situation in the best possible way and that is in line with the company's interests, as well as how to handle the interaction with the specific manager. What are her key objectives? Can HR maybe help you get a grand deal in the headcount game that allows you to share some resource with the manager if she supports your idea?

Tip: give away your marketing personnel allocations and negotiate yourself some more engineers or real sales people (this usually works since nobody likes to do PowerPoint, and marketing people tend to be seen as simple PowerPoint monkeys by most).

Haven't we forgotten something in the HR potpourri? Someone more influential on the success of your venture than anybody else? Yes indeed! Let's talk about YOU! You are a risk — perhaps the greatest risk of them all. And, you are also part of the HR policy, as well as being part of someone's headcount. When making investment decisions, ALL executives will ask the nebulous question: "What do YOU really think about this idea of yours — will it fly?" Based on your immediate response, or lack thereof, the execs will start judging, intuitively or not, on how able you are to perform and execute. Any normal executive will not, of course, generally have the ability or the tools at hand to make a thorough MBTI-style personality analysis. He or she will also probably not say much about you to his or her peers other than "he's a good guy," or "that guy's a real bozo, coming here with a plan like that."

The fact that executives and stakeholders have to judge the elephant-in-the-room risk of betting on you, the budding intrapreneur who could potentially make or break their careers, will be one of the more decisive and least talked about variables in your success. Imagine presenting a great idea to an investment council. You have the best explanations regarding Market and Technology Risk. You have adjusted your business model to fit the grander scheme of the company, and you have a plan to staff up. All questions are answered, right? Yes, and you get the go-ahead from the council.

But remember the headcount game. Consider once again that you are and will belong, even when you get funding for your venture, to someone else's headcount. Now that you have won this investment approval, you will need to be either incubated or absorbed into an existing product line. What will happen if this new manager is not your greatest supporter, since he does not believe in nutty ideas with mad scientists at the helm? Chances are that you will fail because your new manager will decide to sub-optimize your investment dollars in order to fall in line with his greater needs. Or perhaps because he will simply look for a major setback as an excuse to remove you in favor of somebody in his incumbent organization who was promised a promotion in the past. We have seen this happen so many times and it is painful to even think about.

Part of mitigating the above involves working hard on aligning with HR. The reality is that once you have received your investment, you are pretty much on your own. Your progress will be tracked, and you will be asked to show success. You will have to smile all day long and promote yourself and your solution at all times. Simply put, you will need to display and sell yourself 24/7 in order to build a career out of your new internal venture.

Pro Tip

HR is the single most understated resource within the corporate world. HR as a concept should be terminated immediately and replaced by a "Business Scalability Unit" or a "Growth Strategy Unit", or maybe by "Head Count Directors."

The thing is, these roles are totally out of sync with what their titles imply.

Younger people hired for HR roles very often boast degrees and interests that I want the rest of the company to be influenced by: organizational psychology, English lit, finance, and liberal arts. Once hired, they anyway end up destroyed by our corporate process. First they work a few years as "forms robots" and then slowly sink into the role of headcount. At best, they become "talent management" professionals, which is another way of saying they approve trainings. And make sure coffee cups match the number of seats.

Make sure to find yourself the unspoiled gems in your HR department who still have aspirations of one day becoming savvy and creative business professionals. Get these people on your side and get free work done. Bring them into customer meetings and inspire them to help you find the very best employees for this venture. It will pay off!

Chapter 17 - Step 2: Adaptive Communication

A quick search in Amazon's book department for "Communication" generated over 250 000 results. What could we possibly, as simple business guys, add to this sea of opinions and insights?

With all due respect to the "101 Presentation Skills" and "Communicating with Difficult People" authors, these books usually don't cover one really sensitive idea: most corporate communicators pretty much suck, pretty much all of the time. Death-by-PowerPoint meetings happen way too often in corporate settings and seem to be the favored excuse for avoiding real work.

Our take on communication risk in larger companies, if not unique, at the very least involves more than creating great presentations. Not only do many of the presentations on new ventures we see blow donkey privates, but also, many of the presenters are so arrogant that they themselves are the main causes of the inevitable failures of their ventures, regardless of whether their ideas are good. Let us reiterate and rehash that lousy communication and lack of fingerspitzengefühl will inevitably result in failure.

Do you need to have natural ability in business to be the Steve Jobs of your company? To deliver mind-blowing graphics-only notes every single day? Probably not, and in fact, the result if probably the exact opposite. What do you need?

Anchoring. Stand-up comedians use this term when describing a way of quickly getting to know the audience and creating rapport. Everybody loves to hate the way these performers find people to "work with," i.e., ridicule during the show, but doing so is a hallmark of the best comedians. The basic concept is very powerful. You show that you are present with the audience while creating a safe haven that you can return to if you get slightly lost. Even if you bomb, you can still win the crowd as everybody in the audience will be able to relate to you.

Can you imagine anything more personally risky than being the only performer in a stand-up show? You are up there totally naked. If you don't create an instant and lasting rapport with the audience, your 1.5 hours in the spotlight are going to be very painful indeed. So what do good performers do in order to be instantly amazing every night? Simple — they prepare.

Obvious of course, and you must do the same to be great. And here's the thing: there are a few great tricks that you can use to either, as an executive, quickly call the bullshit, or, as a budding intrapreneur, mitigate the risk of getting called out on your weakest spot.

So who is the audience? Everybody you can imagine. That's the whole point. You will have to talk to customers, internal and external stakeholders, your team, top management — everybody. Or at least you should have material ready for all the aforementioned parties. And it will have to be in different forms and shapes, depending on the audience. Remember that short and sweet is not always better, but long and lousy is the worst.

The first core skill you need to develop, and this will be covered in most advanced management books but cannot be emphasized enough, is your ability to tell a story. It should not be goofy or cheesy, but you should be able to return to it in the end to sum up your presentation, and you should start off with it as your elevator pitch. We are not asking you to become a fiction writer (you don't need a story of a lost explorer at sea), but what you do need is a convincing way to talk about the problem you are solving and why the issue is important to the people who are willing to pay. Think of it as the preamble to your great article that explains your venture.

Nowadays, with the proliferation of content sources, everybody is a partial reader of sorts. You're likely thinking, "OK I get it. If I'm creating a photo-sharing app, I should say things like "don't you just hate when you lose a photo? Guess what — our mission is to allow you to share your memories forever with whomever blah blah blah."

Well, not really. But there is always a story. For example, say you have an idea for a new process and software that will shorten the lead-time from supply to delivery by realigning the invoicing process within the heavy truck tires business line. You could say, "I was at a dealer the other day and noticed how they sub-optimized their inventory. I asked them why. Then I asked them why many others did this and was amazed. Just by looking at this small sample, I have found that we could save millions of dollars by investing only a fraction of our overall allocated budgetary spend."

You get the point. Start with the story, every time.

Apart from the story itself, you must create your own anchor point with a specific audience (hint: it's not all about money at the end of the day). We all have things that make us tick, that make us work like ants, like good soldiers. Raises and bonuses are obvious rewards designed to make rational people work harder and more diligently. The assumption is that all we want is more money, an extra buck for an extra mile. And this assumption seems to be correct — why else would managers and salespeople walk the extra mile? Why would they get up in the morning and go to the heavy-duty tire factory? But could there be other intangibles that get people excited?

Yes. Our experience and vast amounts of sociological research tells us that people usually even react better to other incentives, such as recognition, increased responsibility, and the potential to wield greater influence within an organization. What you need to do before presenting your new idea is to find the key to your audience and what resonates with them the most.

Before we give you the lowdown on what you need to do to become the low-risk alternative for middle management, we would like to address a few things that you should never, ever do when presenting to your future stakeholders and customers:

○ Never try to create a sense of urgency by saying that competitors are doing this and that you will be last in the market (unless you are talking in a banking context, where money and envy are the only driving factors of change). Referring to competition and implying that your company is toast unless you get your act together really quickly can backfire severely in a political setting. No manager, especially the manager in charge of the doomed product line, wants his peers and executives to hear that the competition is right and doing so-and-so. You will create immediate antagonism. The incumbent manager, the one who will most likely have to host your venture, since it will be close to her responsibility area, will hate your guts for exposing things she most likely already knew and probably did not want to tell her senior management. In short, you have made her look bad.

○ Never refer to general trends that you have read about on LinkedIn or in your favorite tech blog as evidence of anything, at all...ever. Clearly this is too obvious, isn't it? Still, it is so easy to say things like: "I read that this and that is happening in the market, so we have to be fast." You are setting yourself up here for a major FAIL. There is a high probability that someone else in the room has read the same article. And, what if this person actually knows shit about what the article stated and can kill it with facts? Or maybe that person actually knows the author personally and despises them on an intimate level. You are toast.

○ Never ever expect that creating-another-percent-of-growth-for-the-company is the least bit interesting for a line manager. Don't expect anyone other than perhaps the very top-level managers to be remotely engaged in the greater good of the company. It's a very sad fact and many people will challenge such a statement in public, but yet will secretly agree. As a middle or line manager you are mostly interested in looking good when review season comes up and maybe getting your bonus. What this means is that if you come with a pretentious statement, you will be dismissed as, umm, pretentious. A statement like the "another-percent" early on in your pitch will, without exception, make the rest of the pitch an uphill climb.

So what should you do to become the lowest-risk choice? It is all about risk, isn't it? As we stated earlier in the book, managers in large companies are mainly there to safeguard what is already there. Understand that this is how large companies are set up, with very few, if any, exceptions. Everything from HR processes to financial processes point us in the direction of minimizing the possibility of anybody making too-bold moves and too-crazy bets. But this doesn't mean that some managers in large companies don't try. And this is your chance. There are a few things that you can and should incorporate into your pitch to lubricate the gears of innovation:

- Urgency: this is truly a balancing act. You have to create a sense of urgency, just not in the wrong way. We strongly believe that, in large corporate settings, the chances of achieving a positive decision diminishes exponentially every day and week the decision is delayed. You have to fix this. The very best way of creating urgency in large companies is, ta-da, customer interest. Especially larger customer interest. Large key account manager interest will also sometimes suffice. OK, that's easy then. Just get customers excited. "How the hell do I do that without actually having a product?" Lie! But we will come back to sales later on.

- Recognition: in this context, the term refers to the most common of intangibles. This one very often works, but not if you are too obvious about it. You need to convey the feeling that this venture will make the middle manager get recognized for his extremely insightful and visionary decision to support the young venture. Offer him the possibility of frequently socializing with top management ("what if they see me and make me VP"), the possibility of being interviewed by external sources at industry events ("see me, I'm famous, give me a new job with a VP title, pretty please"), or our very favorite, the possibility of getting his name in a press release that comes up top of the rank when he Googles himself ("I'm searchable for all those headhunters looking for VP candidates — yi-haa"). All of this will be going through the head of this middle manager stakeholder of yours as soon as you show the slide of how hot this area is right now and how many analysts are searching for charismatic leadership in the company in order to enter the scene. The time is now. Fame and VP job titles are waiting.

- The Word of God: so who is your god? Make sure to learn from the church. The corporate god is, of course, the CEO. The chosen one, the one with all the vague answers to specific questions. The guy nobody ever meets but senior managers all refer to by first name — "I ran into Bobby last week and he said that we really need to give this all we got." "Bobby told me that he's really worried about this customer. Better get a move on." And so on. Awful isn't it? Does it work? You bet. And the good part is that you don't even have to meet the guy. All you have to do is find a few good quotations from the latest internal memo, the latest annual report, a YouTube video, whatever. Smack it into your presentation as proof that your idea is exactly what the enlightened one has on his or her mind and be so sure about it that, at the very least, you get the stakeholder thinking of ways to use your venture as an excuse to book a 5 minute meeting with the Emperor, and maybe, maybe, get that VP title.

○ Greater Good: this is arguably the least powerful topic to include if you set out on a tangent explaining why the company NEEDS your venture to show market leadership. But, coming back to how to build your low-risk image, displaying that you are on a passionate mission to solve something difficult is a powerful way to a) prove that you will stick around when the going gets tough and b) entice all the engineers in the room to be part of solving the problem. In engineering companies especially, coming up with a hard problem and a mission to solve it is better than market research — always. If you want people to start calling you and helping you out, that is.

In conclusion: make sure to adapt what you present, depending on your audience; don't piss people off; and make sure that if you want an investment from a senior manager, you make them look good. You want this person to embrace your start-up project because he or she can claim it as a personal win. Yes, sometimes you have to surrender your own ego. Which is also why with some personalities, you will have to back off, even when you know you are right. When you get a push back, pretend to think hard while listening and then change your mind. And always remember to stroke egos with a pitch of subtle praise and reverence. Even if it makes you feel as if you just ate your young.

Pro Tip

Newsflash — you are not a stand-up comedian. You're a person who has been given a break from your mind-numbing corporate job. Don't blow it now. Make sure to thoroughly prepare. Instead of watching yet another rerun of Seinfeld, spend your evening reading up on the people you're going to meet the next day. In fact, get rid of the TV altogether for now and reflect on what you've gotten yourself into and how you're going to win the pitch tomorrow.

And ALWAYS LISTEN, more than you talk. When somebody asks a stupid question, at least pretend to think about the answer for, say, 2 seconds AFTER HE FINISHES TALKING before hammering him with the answer.

Chapter 18 - Step 3: Sell. Sell. Sell.

This chapter is all about our favorite what-they-don't-teach-you-in-business-school-but-should topic. SALES! Which two functions in the company can never go on a 1 month vacation without the company suffering? Sales and operations — everything else is secondary. As a company, you need revenue and products to ship and basically that's it. Everybody else is needed to scale the company, create strategies, do reporting, etc. But at its purest, a company needs money in and products shipped out. In large company settings, where does the most successful marketing professional end up? As VP marketing, at best. Where does the best sales executives end up? As the CEO, CMO or COO (though the finance people are finally catching up). Just look around. More often than not, sales guys run the corporate world.

In Silicon Valley and most other tech-centric start-up environments right now, the product people are the craze. Very often you will hear success case statements such as "We, the core team of smart people, built the product. Then we employed a bunch of sales guys." A bunch of sales guys — how hard can it be? Just get a bunch of them.

Let's dissect this a bit. How exactly does the VP of Product contribute to sales? The typical sales lifecycle is something like this:

> First the sales gal cold calls or meets a customer through her contacts. She endures countless meetings and telephone conversations to convince the prospect not only that the product is something he actually needs, but also that he likes it too.

> The pitch doesn't stop there, of course. The salesperson then has to go through the ultimate humiliation of;

> a) pretending that her refurbished heavy duty truck tire product will change the world forever and;

> b) some young MBA manager tells her that she needs to focus more on the customers' needs, sell the complete solution, and focus less on the problems — "see them as opportunities instead!"

Only after all of this has been done and the customer is really interested will the sales gal bring in the Product Manager. First she wants to make sure that the geeky and introverted Product Manager doesn't screw things up. So she spends weeks preparing the customer for the meeting that should ONLY cover the technical road map and high-level specs.

When the contract is signed, who then spends basically all of his time in the office bragging about the slam-dunk meeting that made all the difference? Right, the Product Manager. Where is the sales gal? With her

RICKARD DAMM   MATTHEW DOERNER-MILLER

customer, of course, firefighting the shitty product that was shipped full of holes.

Exaggerating again? We won't even bother to comment.

So what was the risk again? Aha. The risk is that you, the intrapreneur, are not up for the challenge. Not up for the task. That's it. You will be spending at minimum 80 percent of your time selling. The "corporate tax" you have to pay for leading a relatively exciting and stimulating entrepreneurial life is finding ways to escape to actual customer meetings in between all your internal sales meetings with every stakeholder you could possibly think of.

As the budding entrepreneur, you have the sole responsibility of spreading the word. We have already covered some of the meetings you need to have with HR, and will shortly speak about Finance. In addition, you will pitch to key account managers, admins (yes the admins are really important if you want to get meetings with top execs), R&D managers, developers, janitors — everybody. You will be cold calling internally more that externally. The biggest difference is that internal cold calls usually end with a meeting, which at best will only cost you another hour of real work. So sell like you have a mortgage to pay and 14 hungry kids to feed. Desperation is only the beginning. If you don't pitch all day long, your venture might as well be forgotten right away.

And the single most crucial piece of advice? Remember that it's a give-get world. Give and get. And unless you are the CEO, you are the one who starts — giving that is. You call people and tell them that you can help THEM. You listen to people at the coffee machine and try to help THEM first. Only later do you ask for input on your plan. Never forget this. It's dead easy to let this go once you are the least bit successful. All of a sudden you are that arrogant person nobody wants to help.

Pro Tip

So, now you're the sales guy. You're on the receiving end of this-product-is-a-gift-from-the-gods-that-anybody-can-sell-it comments.

Sales is tough. Boo-hoo. Go cry on the shoulder of some other rank-and-file loser who never bothered to give it a real go. You're in it to the bitter (or successful) end, aren't you? You've come this far; now is not the time to start getting nervous about selling your idea. Go for it!

Being in sales is brutal. It's a numbers game and it's very hard to outsmart the system. Your sales people are on the front lines and are tasked with constant reporting and forecasting; they are the ones requesting money and contracts and the ones who are blamed when things go sour. So give them some slack. Appeal to the fun part of their job — being involved with new products and being part of something that will become amazing. Invite them for dinner for once. Don't get management all fired up without testing your proposition on a couple of senior sales account managers first.

Another thing. When talking to customers, don't forget and don't be afraid to actually ask for money. Even for what you regard as a prototype. Whatever the amount, and no matter your current financial strength, it is always good to have money coming in. Full stop.

Chapter 19 - Step 4: Finance

"Ooh, finance," you say. "This is unexpected and groundbreaking. Let me guess — you want me to create a great P&L that aligns with the finance people. Thanks a lot for the advice."

Yes, we want you to create a great P&L slide and present it to the finance folks. But that's not what we would like to discuss here. We will take you down two paths: one that addresses the actual design of your business model and one that addresses the financial structure of your company and how these two affect the way people act. To put it simply, our aim is to reveal how to influence people to do what you want and to make them understand that it is easier to help you than not. Again we will talk a lot about sales, but this time from the perspective of management accounting and financial steering.

First and foremost your company's structure is inherently formed around how much stuff you sell, period. Sales was most likely the first metric that management tracked ever since the inception of you firm. And, it will also be the last to stay if things go south one day. All other key financial indicators are in one way or other a function of sales. The R&D

budget's size for your new venture, how many product managers can you employ, what is your travel cost ceiling? Outside of the headcount game as discussed earlier, if you look over an extended period of time, your costs will have to be less than what your sales add up to, right? Once you have a grasp of how much you can sell you can also make a good guess of how large the rest of your future organization will be.

You have to be smart with your financial forecasting and design of your venture's business model. You have to make sure your product is sellable within the context of where you are right now. If you nail it you will have money coming in earlier, which in turn will increase your chances of success.

So, let's have a closer look at things to pay attention to and how to get your products sold. How does your company reflect product and business unit performance today? Typically you will hear something such as "# of days outstanding was X, inventory turnover was Y, and the fulfillment rate was Z." It's therefore probably safe to assume that the management accounting and financial systems are set up to measure and support exactly this, correct?

Do managers, shareholders, accountants, banks, and investors all evaluate your company based on your existing business model and performance? Well, they take it into consideration for sure. But your company is mainly priced (by investors) on expected future performance, and this is exactly why new, potentially disruptive ventures are even harder to approve. Nobody knows how they will be perceived by the market and by the analysts. The only thing we know for sure is how these players understand our existing setup, and this equals big risk in the minds of senior managers.

DEATH ON THE BLUE OCEAN

"What? Aren't all managers purposed and conditioned to be "innovation catalysts" and to support "idea generators"? Dream on. Middle management's sole purpose is to safeguard what is already in place, as we've said, and investors like it this way. Before anything else, managers need to make sure that they don't screw up what has been built over decades or even centuries.

"So you're saying that dystopia leads to underinvestment in novel areas as opposed to the innovative culture we always talk about?"

You just earned a cookie. There is a reason why large companies isolate risky (basically all non-incremental) innovations and ventures in "innovation units" or "venture arms." These usually short-lived units have the unenviable task of finding the "next new thing" with limited funding and against all odds. If there ever was a unit in desperate need of some ThirdRisk® thinking, it's the innovation cell.

But what about you, the intrapreneur who needs to navigate through hazy mists of risk — what should and could you do to win over these managerial preservationists?

As boring as it may seem, the first step is to ensure that your venture's business model is designed according to your company's existing business model. Or, at the very least, the core component of your venture should be in line with the overall corporate strategy. This seems rather obvious when you say it aloud, but we feel that this is worth pointing out.

"But isn't the point of doing something new to disrupt what has always been done?" Yes of course, but it makes absolutely no sense to challenge the system if you don't really need to. And the brutal truth is this: it is always, always much easier to adapt your venture to your company's management accounting system than to try to make the system play according to your rules.

Disappointing? Possibly, but your new idea will very seldom totally depend on only one single business and delivery model. Think we are wrong and that we are pushing the limits of acceptable business-book generalization? We beg to differ. Even though your great new idea will totally revolutionize the industry and you have invented the ultimate disruptive business model, you will still have to be smart about it. At the very least, design the core part of your new product to fit with how your company operates today, and then add your smart new ideas as ancillary services later on.

The benefits of adapting and sub-optimizing your venture to be a better systematic fit with your host organization are not unique to you as an intrapreneur. All successful entrepreneurs are able to assess, for example, the strategic health of potential acquirers and financiers. However romantic the idea of being the wild and free entrepreneur creating Facebook in a dorm room and then suddenly dictating financial decisions, the simple truth is that 99.9999 percent of all entrepreneurs are slaves to debt or capital pressures and must become ever-deeply engrained in, for example, the VC's portfolio in order to have at least one single leverage point when money becomes scarce again.

The most important side effect of adapting your corporate venture is this: you will have an improved chance of receiving support from the most influential resource you can possibly have in terms of the success of your project — the sales team! "How is this possible? We already spoke with them, what can those obnoxious people ever contribute to my venture? All they wanted was fame, glory, money, and fame and glory and some more money."

Well here's the kicker, even though we are discussing finance, it is best to return with an example of how the sales team operates and how they get reimbursed for their work. Incentives for sales people are designed to condition these fame-and-bonus-hungry people to, not surprisingly, sell more stuff in the same way they have always sold stuff in the company. Maybe, in very advanced companies, the sales bonuses will also tie in to some sort of Balanced Scorecard approach with a few action-based metrics. But with 99 percent certainty we can say that the bulk of the bonuses will come from selling more of the same compared to last year's results. And it is exactly because of this that you will be able to meet each other in a win-win by adapting your new venture to your company's existing business model.

Imagine that you have not followed our advice and have come armed with a shiny new product and a totally new business model that you will attempt to sell in basically the same way as all other products in the company. Now put yourself in the position of the sales guy you meet in, say, February (Q1 in this specific company) to talk about how your new product is the best thing since sliced bread. The sales guy has just summed up last year's results and has two things on his mind:

1. What do I do with the bonus that will be coming my way soon and
2. How the hell will I make my numbers this year since last year was a mix of luck, magic, and sandbagging.

His targets have just been handed down to him, and, surprise, despite his efforts to explain to everyone of influence that last year was very special, as all his customers upgraded, this year's targets are exactly equal to last year's, plus 10 percent additional growth. Now he's thinking, "maybe I should cancel the order for that new car for my wife, that new house, that new boat. I'll have to live on my bonus when I get FIRED this time next year for not meeting my objectives." You get it right? This is the guy you're meeting.

You present him your new brilliant product and a new and totally complex business model. You'll try to swoon him with grand statements of changing the world and bringing the company into the next phases of growth, yet all he will hear is how hard it will be to sell something so new and that the majority of the revenue generated by his efforts will start to flow into the company in two to three years.

Be proactive here. Present the same product but with a sales-friendly compensation model attached. Charge customers according to a model they are familiar with, and a model that apparently works well enough to have an existing business relationship. Introduce your new and shiny pay-as-you-go business model as a component for parts of the solution. This means that the product will be better aligned with customers' cost targets (e.g. you can probably put some of the normal upfront fees on a variable), and more importantly, your sales reps will be INCENTIVIZED without tweaks to things such as Balanced Scorecards. And with a bit of luck, you might even be seen as the perfect solution to his my-luck-has-run-out issue. If his customers actually bought all they needed last year, he can make his numbers only by selling new stuff. Ka-ching! You and your product pitch are so much better off now.

But why do you really need all of the sales guys on your side anyway?

After all, can't you just launch with partner A and B and do mass email marketing on your own while selling through websites in a pay-as-you-grow model? Won't this be fantastic!

No, it won't. Selling to existing customers is by far the cheapest and fastest way to launch a product. Period. Even if your company only has 100 customers, cross selling is a must. Given that you have a product that is somewhat in line with your company's core, if you can't sell your product to at least one of the company's existing customers on an idea-only basis, chances are you will not be successful with new customers either. This is especially true when considering the aforementioned incentive models and structures of your company.

So, our take on the financial structure of your company goes a little bit deeper than a simple P&L. Everybody operates within a constrained financial system that is, in the near term at the very least, dictated by how your company is run today. It's important to remember that companies are created to make money and provide value (predictable growth) to investors, and planning for this inevitability is your job. Incentives matter — a lot. So do existing customers and relationships. Our example of the sales team incentive structure explains this. Yet sales personnel are not the only ones on the receiving end of being incentivized by how your company operates its financial model. Everybody within the organization is.

Pro Tip

When it comes to the finance reporting side of the house — the actual controlling mechanism of the firm — make sure to find and recruit the best "financial system hacker" you can. This would probably be a seasoned controller in your company who has worked there for ages and knows everyone in the company. Why? When starting a new venture, you will constantly need to chase revenues. And not only chase them, but you will have to steal them back.

When it comes to Excel, do yourself a favor and get to know someone who can prepare RoFo's and sales charts that are a work of art. If you aren't an expert, use someone that is.

A few last and final words from the pro. Remember the Doldrums? It's worth repeating here in the Finance section of the book: If you like requesting unreasonably large upfront investments or need to lie about the market outlook, brace yourself for a bumpy ride down the road.

PART FIVE

K.I.S.S. (Keep It Simple Stupid)

Chapter 20 - Adaptive Business Planning

To get a solid understanding of what constitutes a perceived Market Risk, put on your business development/management consultant hat. Even though you might not have any direct experience in management consultancy, there are plenty of template-based market assessment models out there. And while most are far too simplistic and high-level to help you in any practical sort of sense, you can gain some basic insight into what exactly top management relies on when making decisions.

Senior exec: OK then, can you send me your business plan? I want to take a deeper look into this.

Unprepared You: Right, I was coming to that. Can you give me a few weeks and some money to pay the hotshot consultants we used last time? I mean, we don't want to get the value chain and market estimates wrong

***

Outside of paying for management consultants in the first place (as discussed earlier in the book), adopting the concept of traditional business planning as a way to build your story is the first mistake you can make. Every time you hear someone offer the "advice" of "make a business plan and send it over" — heed Admiral Ackbar's voice in your head. Yes, it is a trap.

You will undoubtedly end up spending far too much time and far too much money on market reports and insights, only to have the plan shot down by even the most infantile of management execs. The business plan is a way for top management to, down the road, hold you hostage by your assumptions, which, by the way, were based on the assumptions of someone else, who in turn probably looked at your company figures or your peers' in the first place, but that's another story altogether.

Every business plan that we have ever seen has been wrong, including our own. Every single one. So where do you go when asked to provide a business plan for your new project?

Here is your first reality lesson in career management: make sure your underlings create the plan and make sure to collectively approve it (at a Steering Committee Meeting, or similar, where no one single manager has any personal decision making traceability), just as long as the numbers reference the large market research houses. No business plan is approved without these figures. Think of unsubstantiated assumptions as a predator and business plans as a pack of wildebeests; the old, slow, and weak ones are easily picked off right away while the rest of the herd spends its remaining days trying to outrun the inevitable — that they too will eventually be the old, slow, and weak.

Let's reverse the odds and hold the senior execs hostage. There is a relatively straightforward way to do this.

Instead of spending weeks on a business plan (or maybe even months), spend a few hardcore days on creating a proper Opportunity Analysis. We know what you're thinking: "So instead of making a real plan, you ask me to make a less worked through plan and call it something else? This is horrible advice!"

Hold on. Yes, you need to do some work. But be smart about it. Concentrate on the "unchallengeable" parts and let the rest be high level. An Opportunity Analysis is a little less all encompassing, a little more distilled. It also comes with an increasingly high level of focus on the actual use cases (i.e. how and will real human beings use your product) and problems you are solving.

An Opportunity Analysis is far more effective in conveying real-time reality. You need to present the following:

1.   Your value proposition and a clear view on what problem you are solving (you are addressing a real problem, aren't you?)

2.   How big the opportunity is

3.   How you plan to test it on real customers

An Opportunity Analysis will give you a feel for how appealing a new product is and how many people out there are willing to pay for it.

You will never pass through any corporate innovation funnel without some sort of market projection. But try making it a bit less macro and a bit more micro. You will still need to present a general market projection slide, but don't spend a disproportionate amount of time dissecting this in detail. Simply find out what your market is and how many people in this market would be willing to pay for a service like yours, i.e., we think that Jane is willing to pay $100, and we think that there are at least 10,000 Janes out there.

A properly developed Opportunity Analysis will also cover your sales and distribution logistics, partnership requirements and opportunities, and of course, the problem you are actually solving. *Gear Up* is a good model that we have used. It covers 9 topics that should be included in an Opportunity Analysis. This model allows you to organize your Opportunity Analysis in a few easy to understand "Gears" (tangents) and build your value proposition accordingly. The *Gear Up* model works very well in larger company settings if augmented with the ThirdRisk® model.

Some final suggestions on the structure of your Opportunity Analysis:

- Tell them what problem you are solving (maximum 2 minutes)
- Show the demo and the product value proposition (take the necessary time needed)
- Dig into the Opportunity Analysis
- Show your technical implementation plan
- Ask for money and tell them how you will use your resources wisely in order to be successful, despite all the nuances of will inside your corporation

Chapter 21 - The Big White Elephant

Corporate "Laws of Nature" are quite often dismissed as being insignificant. Meetings based on changing the company's financial structure or amending the HR policy are thought to be both tedious and minute details. The elephants once again go unreferenced. Raise your hand if you want to be the one who destroys a budding intrapreneur's presentation on how we can create our own corporate "Death Star" and finally dominate the galaxy, by asking a simple question regarding resource availability and potential HR bottlenecks. Trust us, we have tried, and the sound in the room is not as if all of the air has just been sucked out of it. It's the sound as if all of the air has been sucked out and then blown back in through a gigantic whoopee cushion the size of a VW bus.

You: "But with this giant floating spacing station, we will finally be able to overtake the pesky rebels and destroy anyone throughout the galaxy who dare stand in our way."

Us: "OK so you want our company to branch out into the unknown realm of death ray space stations and this will require a team of at least 200 engineers with, what we can see, as needing totally new skill sets. Have you talked to our HR partners about how you will get access to such a talent base? How can you be sure that these people even want to work for a company like ours, and at a reasonable cost? Will this not also impact your growth trajectory? How about the fact that your business model totally conflicts with how our incentive systems are set up - will this not affect how enthusiastic our sales staff will be?"

You get the idea.

Most managers will generally know after the first few slides in your presentation deck if you have been to a training session that taught popular management speak and jargon. In the consultative selling class, or perhaps the adaptive communication class, you were taught to ask probing open-ended questions. This type of pitch usually ends awkwardly, with you asking questions such as, "Tell me more about your problems with A and B." So why did they still show you the door?

Perhaps the developers of the training courses and the authors of the books actually didn't have a clue as to how to run business meetings and create pitches in this day and age? Perhaps the hard and trusted scientific evidence has been outdated since the 1970s? Maybe we have a much more savvy, global, anxious, and intolerant-to-bullshit pedigree of managers today? So how do you address these people then?

In our experience, if you present a way for senior managers to understand, adapt to, and mitigate the risks you are proposing, you will have a much better chance of swaying them.

When we first started our ThirdRisk® model research, we found that a surprising number of failed projects and ventures were given way too much time to ferment before anybody made a deliberate decision about them. Projects, large and small, were hidden away in large corporate budgets and supported by gut feeling–driven managers who very seldom tried to do more than challenge the project's incumbent market projections or technical details.

Even more surprisingly, in most cases (since we mostly work within the context of larger companies), there were more than enough processes to follow along with plenty of very capable key participating stakeholders.

How is it then that still no one saw that the venture would fail from its inception? Someone with a bit of common sense and objectivity should be able to spot the failing venture and raise awareness?

There is a corporate haze and tunnel vision that makes smart people lose their rational instincts and start to believe in fairytales. Groupthink and confirmation bias are two possible explanations commonly accepted when it comes to how people all of a sudden drop their normal logical reasoning skills and fall for the hype.

Again, we know that people win the lottery and that Apple and Facebook are real companies. Divine intervention, luck, and Black Swans could all have a real impact on your venture. But we also know that you will not likely end up at the very tip of the curved hockey stick. This insight, however, should not discourage you from trying. Actually, now that you have come this far in your venture, it is your obligation to persevere.

What you need to do is create the illusion of knowing how to get to the Utopia part of the model. You have to convey that you are the chosen one who can see through the Matrix. You, the intrapreneur, will need to show the senior executives that if they call on you, you WILL ensure that the project comes to fruition. The good thing is that it is actually not that hard, even for the most average of intrapreneurs, to pull off with the 2-by-2 model.

Here's the kicker. In order to make your plan acceptable, plot your path to glory on the 2-by-2 as a curved arrow ending up in the upper right corner — always. You can choose to either sail through the misty archipelago of opportunities in market development or navigate through the high and treacherous seas of technical development towards an existing market. As you know by now, either of these paths comes with its inherent challenges. You should also know which is most appropriate course for you.

Even though you might not have a "reality distortion field", your Strategy, Mission, and Vision Statements need to be bold and dramatic – yet realistic - in order to rally your troops. Becoming the "World Leader in XYZ" will require some very deliberate decisions outside of just building a product and selling it harder that you are today. But yet this is still the basic output of current planning sessions, and if you are trying to match this output with your corporate vision statement, it will certainly not fit. So where do you go from here?

Chapter 22 - Wrapping it Up

All professional and business risks, in one way or another, proportionately map to personal risk exposure. That's why assessing the ThirdRisk® can be really hard sometimes. It quickly becomes personal. Your profession and workplace should be seen as part of a greater socioeconomic system where fabrications like status and social hierarchies are built up over the course of an extended period of time. Everybody knows their place on the social ladder, yet maintaining and maneuvering your grip on its rungs is a dangerous necessity. In failing with your internal venture and becoming the persona non grata in your ice cream factory, you run the very real risk of being personally affected by losing your influence internally, or even worse, your job completely. You are now the guy who couldn't even successfully launch a new ice cream flavor – how hard can it be?

Making an investment proposal for a new venture is risky, for you personally, whether you like it or not. But this is also part of the thrill with being the corporate entrepreneur. So, after reading this far in our book, do you still believe that the main purpose of the Balanced Scorecard or the rolling forecast is to help you achieve those big hairy goals, or to ensure alignment with the company's long term strategy and provide a means by which senior executives can monitor you and your team?

What purpose does a risk assessment serve in your business plan? Is it there to help you mitigate your risks effectively or can it be used against you when/if things go south later on?

After reading this far in our book do you still believe that the main purpose of the Balanced Scorecard or the rolling forecast is to help you achieve those big hairy goals, or to ensure alignment with the company's long term strategy and provide a means by which senior executives can monitor you and your team?

What purpose does a risk assessment serve in your business plan? Is it there to help you mitigate your risks effectively or can it be used against you when/if things go south later on?

Setting the scene: It is now 2 years after your initial launch and you are in need of additional funding. Targets were missed and your managers are on the war path.

Senior executive: "I see that in your original risk assessment you highlighted the risk of customers opting for cheaper and less functionally-advanced solutions. Maybe this is the reason for your missed sales and customer acquisition targets? What did you do to mitigate this?"

Thinking that he actually had read that in your original report 2 year ago, you are now caught off guard that he is challenging you with this now.

Crickets.

Of course the senior executive did not read it at that time. In fact he just searched his mailbox 15 minutes before this meeting, having privately already decided that you were going to be replaced by the turnaround guy. He just need some ammunition and found it hiding in the dusty risk assessment.

Why didn't someone say something smart when reading your risk assessment the first time? Why when I received all of the originally requested funding did nobody bother to ask how much I would reserve for these type of situations?

Outside of the business plan being a trap, remember, generally speaking, identifying, assessing and presenting Market and Technology Risk within the framework of a traditional business plan will be the dullest part. At the very inception of a new venture, neither you, your executives, or your team want to spend any time or money on mitigating for risks that might happen 2 years down the road. Adding a ThirdRisk® assessment to this equation will not wow your crowd either. Which is why at the point in time when you are heading into make or break meetings, that dumb your message down even further.

A child's mind is inquisitive, but this inquisitiveness is usually accompanied by a very, very short attention span. Children are eager to take in vast amounts of information because they want to immediately venture out and act upon it. They want to know enough, but only just enough to be able to take action.

If this sounds strangely familiar, it's probably because many of your company's decision makers are similar to children in this regard. They do not want to receive emails the length of PhD dissertations, nor do they want overly complicated narratives during presentations. While this presentation may be your first meeting in a week, a month, or even a year, they've already sat through 5 on this day alone, and probably have another 2 on deck. Think of yourself as the 500th solo-act-guitar-strumming-falsetto-upper-middle-class-teenager in their *American Idol* judging tour. So do yourself an immediate favor: dumb down the technical lingo and detailed functional specifications and get to the point. If they are interested, they will follow up with these types of information requests. Salesmanship 101 — make them come back to you.

A bit exaggerated, we know, but the point is that you need to abstract your story into something understandable and easily demonstrable. Which by the way, is not something everyone can do.

For example, take the technical part of your presentation. Make sure to have a really good "technical cofounder" who can abstract it for you in case you can't do it yourself. Worst case (or best), depending on how you see it, is to just present a compelling drawing or a piece of cardboard accompanied by a description of the user experience and the end user value proposition. Seeing is believing, remember.

After this, explain the underlying technology in layman's terms, and keep the detailed slides hidden for later. Too many excited engineers have tried to wow their audiences by their fantastic knowledge of everything nerd. Remember that most of your senior managers were at one point probably up to date with the latest coding and development techniques but haven't actually used these skills in a long time. Worse yet, some might have come from different industries altogether. Salesmanship 102 — always make the receivers of your message feel smart and secure in their knowledge base. Never make them feel as though they are the only ones who don't get it.

Continue on with a 30-, 60-, and 90-day plan of how you'll validate your technology according to your technical team's assumptions. Do not create a technical implementation proposal that cannot be verified, at the very least in parts, within a 90-day timeframe. We can promise that if you create anything that will take beyond three months to even get working in the smallest of its individual parts, you're toast.

The Opportunity Analysis and ThirdRisk® are covered in earlier chapters. But the same goes for them. Dumb it down. That's our final piece of advice.

The importance of enhancing one's skills in corporate entrepreneurship cannot be overstated. Yet due to the corporate ignorance that permeates most traditional companies today, the true importance of intrapreneurs goes unnoticed. Countless examples exist of people successfully starting a corporate venture only to be ousted or "transitioned" into some other start-up project once the product starts to gain traction.

Corporate "bullying" occurs all the time. Call it human conditioning, Corporate Darwinism, or passive aggressive jealousy — whatever it is, the outlier is rarely regaled within corporations today, despite the internal press releases to the contrary.

The truth is that even if you have the best-executed venture, you will be seen as either the mad scientist or the career-failure guy when asking for your next new position. Why is this? Why are there very few quality "entrepreneur in residence" programs for good intrapreneurs? We could easily invest in strategic management planning programs that in turn invest in high-caliber people and task them to run new ventures; succeed or fail, they would be taken care of. We could actually realize that some people are entrepreneurial producers rather than administrators/ integrators. These people should run things through the idea phase and be replaced by true "scalers" a year or so in. And the inventors should receive company-wide recognition to encourage others to actually "Think Big" and not simply hang posters on their walls expressing the mantra.

We cannot stress enough the importance of having a successful career in a large company, despite a failed venture. Statistically, chances are that you will fail. How does your company handle people with multiple failures in their pockets when planning and recruiting for that next-generation-high-potential-managers course and program? This career aspect of the ThirdRisk® is really the very essence of corporate risk. If people saw risk taking being rewarded, or at the very least not punished, idea output would exponentially increase. People would inevitably embrace change to a greater extent and operate with a greater level of support and collaborative understanding towards one other.

CFO: This training costs too much. We can't give it to all the employees. What if they quit?

CEO: What if we don't give them the training, and they all stay?

Do you really want to work in this company? Do you really believe, truly, that this company will achieve greatness by going about its incremental improvements?

The corporate game is a tricky one to play, especially in this day and age. Many simply feel lucky to have a paycheck coming in every month and have little desire to brandish the sword of change with a new product or idea. We get this, and this is ok. We have families to support and bills to pay too. But try to think about it in a different way. What if you never give yourself the chance to prepare for such a moment and the moment suddenly finds you? What if, in your attempt to keep your head down and play it safe, you were called upon to take the lead in finding and pitching a new idea or product? After all, your steady and responsible work within the firm has assured upper management that you are the best steward for their new corporate entrepreneurial initiative. By keeping your head down and not beating the drum for constant change, you may have actually backed yourself into the corner and increased the likelihood that you will be called upon. And what if your very ability to support your family and pay your bills depends on how you respond to this challenge?

This book is not meant to kick down doors and break all other frameworks into teeny tiny irrelevant pieces. It is meant for people like us — average Joes who simply want to excel and manage corporate expectations if and when we are called upon. So the next time you receive an internal memo from management emphasizing "corporate excellence" and "being more entrepreneurial," take a breath, share a laugh, and trust that this handbook and the ThirdRisk® framework will guide you through.

Epilogue

Alexander Tolliver awoke with a start. Each raindrop from the small cluster of clouds above felt like a tiny needle prick on his cracked lips and blistered skin. Although surrounded by water, this was the first real moisture his body had felt in seven long nights at sea. He remained on his back on the bottom of his battered boat and contemplated if he should say a prayer for the midnight shower to increase in strength, casting him into the sea for good, or if it should never end and allow him to gather enough strength for a another day of floating. He could not decide.

Tolliver had run the series of events that had led him to this fate for every waking minute of every waking hour of every waking day. As the first days had passed for Alexander, his maddened mind had laid blame at the feet of everyone else but himself. His financiers were too greedy, his crew too casual. He had allowed passengers aboard that had no business being present, and the maps that he had secured were obviously outdated. He had been let down by all involved.

But as the quiet rain began to lay softer on his skin, a realization began to take shape. Alexander Tolliver understood that the blame was really only his to hold. He had allowed himself to become swayed and influenced by his financiers and passengers. When planning for this voyage he could never have imagined the type of political pressures and subsequent unrest that would ensue, although now it seemed so very obvious. He did not own the company that had supplied him his ship, nor did he invest any of his personal finances. He had been simply so very excited to have received an opportunity to fulfill his dreams of exploration that he never took these factors into account. He had failed in his planning, and only now did he recognize his fatal error.

The moon had risen full and hard. The small clouds above were now empty, and the stars smiled into the sea still as glass. Tolliver swore to himself that although it was the deepest hour of night, that he had never seen a place so full of light and brightness.

He found the stars from his childhood off in the distance. They were at a different angle to be sure than what his homeland's shoreline revealed, but they were there all the same. And yet now another light shone along the water that was unlike both the stars and moon above. A tiny pin of yellow flickered far off in the distance and reflected itself off of the completely still surface.

Tolliver sat up and placed himself onto the waterlogged bench of the tiny rowboat. He reached down and picked up its oars, unused for nearly the entire time afloat, and placed the paddles into the water. This dream of his had not died, nor had he failed absolutely in his attempt to secure it. His current situation was merely a side note – a small distraction – to where he really was headed as an explorer and adventurer. He would not be defined by this one moment.

Alexander Tolliver's body felt as light and as rested as it had in days, and with a quiet, happy sigh, he began to slowly yet steadily paddle towards his salvation.

DEATH ON THE BLUE OCEAN

Endnotes

Failure rates of startups:

Information and Observations on State Venture Capital Programs, Report for the U.S. Department of the Treasury, Cromwell Schmisseur LLC, 2013

http://www.geekwire.com/2012/hard-truth-report-75-percent-startups-fail/

The Venture Capital Secret: 3 Out of 4 Start-Ups Fail, Deborah Gage, WSJ, 2012

Managing Technical risk:

Managing Technical Risk: Understanding Private Sector Decision Making on Early Stage, Technology-based Projects. 2000. http://www.atp.nist.gov/eao/gcr_787.pdf

Taking Technical Risks: How Innovators, Managers, and Investors Manage Risk in High-Tech Innovation. Lewis M. Branscomb, Philip E. Auerswald. 2003. The MIT Press

Market Risk:

The Four Steps to the Epiphany: Successful Strategies for Products that Win. Steve Blank. Cafepress.com. 2005.

Gear Up your best Business idea ever. Lena Ramfelt, Jonas Kjellberg, Tom Kosnik. 2012

The Lean Startup: How Today's Entrepreneurs Use Continuous Innovation to Create Radically Successful Business, Eric Ries, Crown Business, 2011

Disruption:

Michael E. Raynor, "Disruption theory as a predictor of innovation success/failure", Emerald 39, (2011)

The Innovator's Manifesto: Deliberate Disruption for Transformational Growth. Michael Raynor. Crown Business. 2011

Rogers, E. M. (2003). Diffusion of innovations (5th ed.). New York: Free Press.

The Toyota Hybrid case:

http://www.ae.pwr.wroc.pl/filez/20110606092430_HEV_Toyota.pdf

http://money.cnn.com/magazines/fortune/fortune_archive/2006/03/06/83 70702/

http://www.automobilemag.com/features/0712_hybrid_history/viewall.ht ml

The High tech innovator case

Internal material and sources

Employee engagement:

A little more conversation, a little less information. Richard Donkin, WSJ, 2005. http://www.ft.com/cms/s/0/60ad1f82-3085-11da-ba9f-00000e2511c8.html#axzz2cjHLO2UN

WELL-BEING: FIELD-TESTED COMMUNICATIONS STRATEGIES THAT ENGAGE EMPLOYEES, Stein and Beaudin-Klein, HealthPartners 2012

CHA PR Report. A little more conversation: Employee Communications Approaches and Their Impact, London, 2005

Blue Ocean Strategy:

Kim, W. Chan; Mauborgne, Renée (1 February 2005). Blue Ocean Strategy: How to Create Uncontested Market Space and Make Competition Irrelevant. Harvard Business Press.

Kim, Chan (2005). Blue Ocean Strategy. Boston: Harvard Business School Press. pp. 210–211. ISBN 1-59139-619-0

DEATH ON THE BLUE OCEAN

ABOUT THE AUTHORS

Rickard Damm

 With a background from senior management positions in large blue-chip multinationals such as General Electric and Ericsson, Rickard has a solid track record of building successful businesses in multiple regions throughout the world.

Rickard has extensive experience in portfolio management, sales, strategic business development, project management, contract negotiations, leadership and customer services on a global scale.

Rickard's business experience ranges from medical devices, telecom and digital media. Most of Rickard's professional career has gravitated around turnarounds, M&A and start-up businesses within large organizations.

Rickard has a Diploma and an MBA from the Stockholm School of Economics. He is frequently engaged as a speaker, advisor and thought leader within telecoms, media, internet and web trends. He currently lives in Nacka, just outside central Stockholm with his wife and three sons.

Contact details: rickard.damm@gmail.com or through LinkedIn

Matthew Doerner-Miller

Although currently in the banking and finance industry, Matthew's old life of "all things start-up" extended to both web-based IT start-up enterprises as well as more traditional brick and mortar businesses.

With extensive first-hand experience in the establishment of business enterprises throughout Latin America, the Caribbean, Canada, Europe and the United States, Matthew's working knowledge of the intimacies and intricacies of managing and developing ventures within a global marketplace is vast.

He holds a BA Honors degree from the University of Western Ontario as well an MBA from the Stockholm School of Economics.

Contact details: mdoernermiller@gmail.com or through LinkedIn

www.ingramcontent.com/pod-product-compliance
Lightning Source LLC
Chambersburg PA
CBHW051506170526
45166CB00001B/413